# Enterprise Data Architecture:

## How to navigate its landscape

Published by Paragon Publishing

ISBN 978-1-78222-326-9

Revised 2018

Book design, layout and production management by Into Print

www.intoprint.net

+44 (0) 1604 832149

# Contents

# This book provides a simple, easy to follow guide, describing what needs to be understood, in order to deliver more from Enterprise Data Architecture.

This is quite an ambitious claim, because how could an Enterprise Data Architecture book that is less than three hundred pages long, possibly compete in usefulness with a tome defining a framework's minutiae?

What it cannot know are: your personal characteristics, your experience to date, and the challenges that you face. In that case, how can it possibly help you?

Well, I believe it can.

If Enterprise Data Architecture is about anything, it is about principles and patterns. But of course, it shares this characteristic with *all Enterprise* Architecture.

The thing that distinguishes Enterprise Data Architecture, is that it needs to provide the maximum benefit to an organisation from its data, over extended periods of time.

In order to do this, it needs to transcend the buffeting caused by the continual upheavals in the world of data. This includes, of course, those due to the emergence of the Cloud, Big Data and more recently AI, and Machine Learning. In order to provide this constant benefit in a totally variable landscape, there needs to be something that remains constant about Enterprise Data Architecture.

My aim in writing this book is to explain these constants, and the way to think about them.

If this interests you, then this is the right book for you.

The central question that it must answer is; how can Enterprise Data Architecture preserve an organisation's data benefit despite the relentless barrage of change that assails most organisations today?

The answer is that Enterprise Data Architecture must be based upon certain *immutable* principles. These will act as a guide to all decision making in this malleable landscape. This approach is not the same as defining a framework, since it must be abstracted at a level above any frameworks. The reason for this is that frameworks will be adopted, adapted and ultimately discarded.

Enterprise Data Architecture needs to make an organisation's data resilient to even these passing perturbations.

Satellite navigation products provide a good metaphor for the way this book is intended to be used. Frameworks are analogous to maps. They describe the rigid formation of structures within which to carry out work. That is their strength and that is why organisations embrace them. They bring a predictability of standards, guidelines and patterns that attempt to thwart individual interpretations of the way things should be done.

Whilst there is a lot of benefit to this, and it works well for large organisations, it is not the way that this book wants you to think about data.

Instead, it will describe ways of looking at the world that will allow you to work within *any* framework. But using defined thought-processes and techniques that will help you to enhance what can be delivered.

As a result, it delivers a guide to the concepts, skills and techniques, as well as ways of looking at Enterprise Data Architecture that will allow you to:

- determine where you are now

- define where you want to be

- establish an optimal navigation route between the two

- optimise any detours that occur on your journey due to unforeseen circumstances

So now it becomes a little clearer why on the cover of this book is a phone with a satellite navigation system, and why its title includes 'How to navigate its landscape'.

The way that satellite navigation systems achieve analogous objectives, is by using in-built behaviours that create one or more optimised potential routes. There is also real time data streaming into them about their current location, and possible impediments to progress, such as: slowly moving traffic, incidents or road works.

The system provides optimised routes taking all of the constraints into account. Even if you take a wrong turning, it will create a new route, allowing you to still reach your original destination.

By contrast to a satellite navigation system, in the Data Architect's view of the world, almost *nothing* is fixed!

Not the:

- starting point

- destination

- landmarks

- road network or even the

- vehicle that they are travelling in!

This means that the Data Architect needs to have *internalised models* built from a set of *constant principles* that can be applied to their world of constant change.

A set of such guidance principles is included throughout the book. These principles are the ones that I have found repeatedly useful when having to make decisions within the scope of Enterprise Data Architecture.

---

*Principle 1*   ***Architectural Principles are the most basic building blocks that provide rigour and coherence to Architectural thought.***

---

The principles are included with the formatting style as in principle 1. Appendix A includes the consolidated set of principles with their corresponding page references.

## Who Are You?

If you are interested in improving the benefit an organisation can derive from its data use, then this book has been written with you in mind.

Although it is written with an emphasis on the Data Architect role, it is equally applicable to many other roles involved with data, for example, you might be a:

- COO looking to get a clear, big-picture view of data and how it can be used to improve operations

- CDO trying to bring order to the current state of your data

- CIO wanting to understand how to derive the most benefit from a transformation programme

- Business Analyst wanting to make sure that requirement definitions fit into a coherent data picture

- Software Engineer trying to produce components that serve the organisation better, both for the immediate *and* longer terms

The content has been written with an expectation that, even if you don't have extensive experience of systems and delivery methodologies, you are at least aware of their features. Better yet, of course, if you do have some direct experience.

However, its emphasis on the strategies and practical steps towards success, rather than the minutiae of code check-ins, will make it useful for those with little technical background.

Whoever you are, and whatever your reason for reading this book, I sincerely hope that it will bring real benefits to you, and to the organisations within which you work.

Dave Knifton

# 1: Data And The Real World

*Our understanding of data facilitates all areas of collective human endeavour — but what exactly is it?*

The purpose of this book is to explain how Enterprise Data Architecture can provide an organisation with the maximum possible benefit from its use of data.

But before we can understand how to achieve this goal, we need to get back to basics and create a handful of very simple definitions of data and its relationships with organisations. It is the job of this first chapter to describe these.

As we progress through the subsequent chapters, we will use these definitions to provide a firm basis on which we can build more advanced concepts.

Fundamental to all of the concepts is the recognition that the exchange of data's *meaning* provides the basis for *all* our organisations' interactions and operations. It is this meaning of the data that allows us to understand the activities that take place in the operational Real World of our organisations. This is not only true for the internal organisational interactions and operations, but also those that take place into the external environment in which it operates.

The interactions and operations may be triggered by activities and/or act as triggers for other activities. Since these activities determine the way that an organisation interacts with its data, the organisation must evolve an effective function that understands them and is also able to exercise direct, positive control of them. This function is called its Enterprise Data Architecture.

Because these activities vary from organisation to organisation, the Enterprise Data Architecture function must be created and continue to evolve to be responsive to the culture and needs of its organisation.

Part of this responsiveness can be successfully achieved by using some very simple standard techniques. Underpinning these, is the principle that to maximise beneficial outcomes from *any* endeavour, it is critical to align all of its component parts.

In this chapter, we will introduce some simple models that will help us to visualise these ideas and other concepts relevant to the meaning of data and its communication.

## What Is Data?

Over the years, I have read a lot of explanations of data and its relationship with organisations, but what exactly is it?

At its very simplest, we can think of data as providing a description of the Real World in a way that allows us to make sense of it.

*Principle 2*     ***Data reveals the truth about what is going on in the Real World.***

Within this definition of data, are *transactions* that record events and their outcomes. In themselves, the data describing the events and their outcomes are meaningless.

**Figure 1 – Data without Meaning**

In the example in figure 1, the data value **750** has magnitude, but we cannot make any sense of it. It *means* nothing to us.

It is only when we create a *definition framework* to provide a context for it that its *meaning* can be understood. This determines that to deliver benefit from our data, we *must* create a meaning framework around it.

**Figure 2 – Data with meaning**

In the example in figure 2, we immediately see that adding a simple meaning framework to the value, results in it being placed into a context that allows us to fully understand its significance.

> *Principle 3*    ***Data can only have meaning and therefore provide benefit for us, when we construct a meaning definition framework around it.***

## Meaning in Data

The exchange of data's *meaning* provides the basis for all interactions and operations; both throughout an organisation, and externally into the environment in which it operates. Yet many times in discussions about data definitions, it seems as if the meaning of data is somehow an optional extra.

How many times do we hear variations of this snippet?

'Oh don't worry about what it's called, I'll put something in for that later ...'

Unfortunately, for organisations, this 'meaning as optional extra' approach is unacceptable. This is because, these *meanings* constitute the very core of an organisation's interactions with its data.

The *meaning* of data is *almost* everything, but in fact there is a nuance we need to add, which the following principle indicates.

---

**Principle 4**    *For organisations, the universally understood and agreed meaning of data is everything.*

---

This principle reinforces the importance of the relationship between data and the organisation making use of it.

This relationship must be embodied and maintained within a specialised function of the organisation, as described in the next section.

## The Enterprise Data Architecture function

The Enterprise Data Architecture function exists to produce the maximum possible benefit to an organisation from its data use, as described in principle 5.

---

**Principle 5**    *The purpose of an organisation's Enterprise Data Architectural function, is to maximise the benefit it derives from its data.*

---

This maximum benefit can only be achieved if Enterprise Data Architecture creates alignment of data interactions across the organisation, as stated in principle 6.

> *Principle 6*     *In order to maximise the benefit for an organisation's strategies and day to day operations, Enterprise Data Architecture must align the production, modification and consumption of its data.*

To maximise the benefit of the data that flows *across* an organisation, the shared definitions must have an Enterprise-wide view.

## Enterprise Data

In order to derive the maximum benefit from its data for the entire organisation, there must be *consistent meaning* applied to it - *across all* parts of the organisation.

> *Principle 7*     *The definition of data that flows across an organisation, needs to have an Enterprise-wide view in order to maximise its benefit.*

If the collective understanding of data can be agreed across an organisation, then we consider it to be Enterprise Data.

> *Principle 8*     *We can consider data to be Enterprise Data, if the uniformity of its meaning can be agreed across an organisation.*

There is another more subtle, and often ignored aspect to this shared *meaning*, and this is to do with the stakeholders involved in its use.

To maximise the data's benefit to an organisation, all of the organisation's stakeholders must *share* the *universally agreed definitions* of the data.

---

**Principle 9**   *The meaning of data can only truly be of Enterprise significance, if all the organisation's stakeholders share the same definitions of it.*

---

In other words, what people in one part of an organisation think a 'Client Account Authority' means, should be exactly the same as what someone from a totally different area thinks it means[1].

We must consider how this is achievable in our organisations, as without effective dissemination of the definitions of our data, its effectiveness will always be compromised.

Immediately, sharing the meaning of our data raises the question of communication.

When considering meaning and communication, it is useful to consider relevant conceptual frameworks to improve our understanding, for example:

- Semiotics

- Discourse Analysis

Both of these fields of study have at their core, the premise that communication messages are composites of:

- content and

- meaning

This premise is entirely consistent with the preceding definitions of data's meaning but also emphasises that meaning is not a static thing; it is the critical component of *communication flows*. Therefore, we need to consider some characteristics of the way that data is communicated throughout an organisation.

---

1    With the caveat that they may use synonymous terms.

## Communication Mediation

Since operations within an organisation depend primarily on organisational data flows, if these flows are inadequate, inappropriate or impaired, this will have a detrimental impact on the effectiveness of the organisation.

> ***Principle 10***     ***To operate optimally, organisations must establish and maintain optimal data flows.***

The *meaning* of data in communication flows is absolutely key for its consumers.

It is important to note though that the data's meaning is mediated due to the dissemination mechanisms and a complex set of the recipient's characteristics. For people, for example, this mediation can including factors such as: experience, knowledge, culture and gender.

Mediation has a direct impact on the shared meaning of data, and Data Architects must therefore consider how to mitigate this potentially negative impact.

The following simple schematic illustrates this concept.

**Figure 3 – Simple communication mediation model**

Figure 3 shows that messages are not absolutes, but are mediated through their communication mechanisms.

> **Principle 11**  *The mitigation techniques used to overcome an audience's possible mediation of the meaning of messages, are key factors for effective communication throughout the organisation.*

The data flows of communication referenced in principle 11, could involve any mechanisms including: emails, documents, presentations, dashboards or system flows. The same simple principle applies to them all.

Ways in which it is possible to mitigate the mediation effects of communication are explored repeatedly throughout this book.

The Data Architect should be considered as a key component in the organisation's operations, and therefore must be an active part of the organisation's communication network. This means that if they are to be successful, they must be effective communicators.

However, data flows need to come from *somewhere* and therefore we naturally need to consider the accessibility challenges of data.

## Known and Shareable Data

'*Known*' and '*Shareable*' represent two important characteristics of data's availability that need to be critically assessed when proposing its use.

These terms challenge the ease with which data can made available and useful to an organisation. The outcomes from these challenges should be used to judge the achievability of proposed benefits from requirements.

Let's look at exactly what is meant by these two terms.

### Known

We are constantly immersed in data.

Some of it is *Known* and what we mean by this is that it is *recorded somewhere*.

> **Principle 12**      *Whether data is Known, provides a challenge to the assumption that it is recorded somewhere, even if fleetingly.*

That 'somewhere' is the interesting bit, for instance, the data may be known:

- in someone's head

- on a yellow sticky on someone's monitor

- in a shared spreadsheet

- in an organisation's Supply Chain Management (SCM) system

The preceding examples illustrate the characteristics of data that pass the *Known* test, but the *Shareable* test applies further challenges to it.

## Shareable

Even if data is *Known,* is it *Shareable?* What we mean by this is to challenge how *easily data can be shared outside of its Known domain.*

Therefore, data that is *Shareable*, is not isolated to the domain in which it is *Known.*

> **Principle 13**      *Whether data is Shareable is an assessment of how easy it is to use it outside of its Known domain.*

Even if it is held in an organisation's SCM system and therefore apparently *Shareable*, this is not necessarily the end of the challenge. For example, here are a number of challenges that can be applied to the *Known* data contained in the earlier SCM example:

1   What technological and organisational obstacles need to be overcome

before the data can be sourced?

    a. Is the SCM system under the direct control of *this* organisation?

    b. Even if the SCM is under the control of *this* organisation, is it isolated in its own data silo?

2  Are there any restrictions on the data to do with Data Hosting or Data Privacy?

3  What are the costs associated with gaining access to the data?

4  What are the data transfer aspects such as frequency of data acquisition?

5  How stable are its Reference Data domains, and are they aligned with those of the organisation?

And possibly the most important question of all, is to ask 'Do We Care?'

## The 'Do We Care?' Test

The most important test for *any* work carried out within the scope of a Data Architect is the 'Do we care?' challenge. The application of this test can eliminate wasted effort in areas where there is in fact little or no realisable benefit for the organisation.

---

**Principle 14**    *Only activities whose potential outcomes pass the 'Do we care?' test, are worthwhile devoting resources to.*

---

Any effort that would otherwise be wasted, can be redirected to other activities that will produce greater benefit from it.

The 'Do we care?' test should be applied by the Data Architect to all proposed activities. This challenge will allow them to optimise their effort and hence achieve the maximum outcomes from their work.

The mantra of this challenge will recur throughout this book, and therefore demands that we understand a little more about how to model effort and benefit for organisational activities.

## Organisations' Activities

Let's consider the events that initially create the data, and subsequently modify it through its lifecycle.

We have already mentioned that data records the changes associated with events within the organisation's realm, for example, 'Receipt of a Payment'. These events are themselves largely driven, and responded to, by *activities*.

To derive the maximum benefit from its data, it is therefore critical to understand an organisation's activities. This is because they define the way that an organisation *interacts* with its data. Understanding this, will allow us to define the events and related data states. Hence, we can create the corresponding framework of meaning.

> *Principle 15*  *Only by understanding the activities required by an organisation, can we fully understand how data underpins its operations.*

## Activities in Successful Organisations

For organisations that wish to thrive in today's turbulent world, it is essential for them to become agile. Arguably, with the constantly increasing pace and pressures for change, any organisations that are unable to become agile, will not survive for very long.

By agile, we mean that the organisation is able to rapidly and successfully adapt to change with minimal effort and disruption. As an overarching principle, this means that all effort must be effective and create negligible waste.

This echoes the 'Do we care?' challenge of before, and brings the concept of *wasted* effort into sharp relief.

When attempting to reduce waste in activities, we need to focus on comparing what *is* done, with what *needs to be* done. A simple model of this concept is illustrated in figure 4.

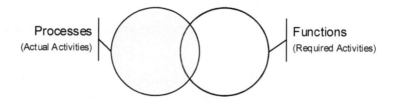

**Figure 4 – Actual activities versus required activities**

Highly successful organisations make sure that what they *are* doing, is exactly what they *should* be doing. They also ensure that they stop expending effort on worthless activities.

Obviously, the lower the degree of overlap of the two sets of activities in figure 4, the more opportunity there is for an organisation to re-engineer its Processes, and thus improve its effectiveness.

We will repeatedly return to this idea of re-engineering an organisation's processes, to see how we can significantly reduce waste using architectural approaches. However, because of the importance of activities in defining data, we will consider how to mentally model them in more detail in the next sections.

## Processes

Processes describe the activities that are *actually* carried out by an organisation.

---

**Principle 16**    *Processes define what activities an organisation actually carries out.*

---

Process definitions are specified within the context of the way that the organisation carries out activities today. As a result, today's *mechanisms* typically become embedded into their definitions. What we mean by the term 'mechanism', is the physical way that an activity is carried out. For example:

**'Email the Client to confirm receipt of their Order'**

## Functions

By contrast to Processes, Functions are *abstracted* definitions of the activities that an organisation *should* carry out, in order to be successful now *and into the future*.

---

*Principle 17*   ***Functions are abstracted definitions of activities that an organisation needs to perform, in order to survive and thrive into its future.***

---

Because these activity definitions are abstracted, they should not make references to any specific mechanism that *could* be used to carry them out. So instead of 'Email the Client to confirm receipt of their Order', an equivalent Function would specify:

**'Confirm the receipt of the Order with the Client.'**

In fact, we can think of these as *'idealised* Processes', that is, they purely describe *what* activities *need to be carried out*, but are totally agnostic to the *way that they are actually carried out*.

## Organisation Fitness

Let's apply the contrast between Functions and Processes to provide a simple model for assessing the fitness of an organisation.

A simple way of measuring the fitness of an organisation is to compare what it *actually does* with what it *should be doing*. Processes that either partially, or wholly, have no corresponding Functional equivalent, represent waste. These are therefore good candidates for either redefining, or removing entirely.

Where Functions have no Process equivalents, effort should be devoted to their implementation. This will add to the organisation's capabilities and allow it to operate more effectively.

> **Principle 18** *If sufficient effort is devoted to all of the activities that it should be doing, and hardly any to activities of little benefit, then the organisation can be thought of as very fit.*

## Business Process Re-engineering

The principle behind Business Process Re-engineering, is to improve an organisation's fitness, by modifying its operations in a way that will yield greater benefit from the activities it performs. It does this through a managed realignment of Processes to more accurately reflect the *required* Functions. It also removes *redundant* Processes and wasteful mechanisms.

## Do we care?

Hold on! What has any of this to do with Data Architecture and Data Architects? After all we are Data folk not Function folk!

Although Data Architects need not be concerned with Function versus Process per se, as a foundational principle, they should ensure that solutions are future-proofed against changes caused by the re-engineering of underpinning Processes.

This is because in a bid to re-engineer an organisation's Processes to be more efficient, mechanisms may need to be replaced. If solution definitions are resilient to such mechanistic changes, then we will improve the overall agility of our organisations.

> **Principle 19** *To make them more resilient to any changes in mechanisms, solutions should be based upon abstracted Function definitions, rather than mechanistic Process definitions.*

This is, of course, not always possible, and some mechanistic definitions may be mandated. For example, mechanisms can be prescribed due to legislative or regulatory requirements.

## Organisation Awareness

Now we have looked at Processes and Functions as a way of conceptualising an organisation's operational activities, let's consider the stakeholders within the organisation.

An organisation's relationships with its data are (still) largely established through its stakeholders. Therefore, we need to consider how they are involved in the definitions of our data.

### Awareness Model of an Organisation's Activities

Typically, everyone who works for an organisation is aware of their relationship with it. They are also familiar with at least some of the other stakeholders, and their relationships with it.

As a result, in the head of every stakeholder of an organisation, is a complex set of knowledge, behaviours, expectations and value judgements. These are about, the organisation, the way that it operates and, in particular, the way that it relates to the individual stakeholder.

> *Principle 20*  *The set of a stakeholder's complex personal attributes, can be thought as their Awareness Set.*

We can consider a simple visual representation of an individual employee's Awareness Set, as illustrated in figure 5.

**Figure 5 – Individual Awareness Set model**

This employee works alongside a colleague on a day to day basis. As a result, their individual Awareness Sets have a large degree of overlap. The two individuals report to a supervisor who knows something about what they do, and how they do it, but does not know all of the detail.

However, the supervisor, does have knowledge about the way the organisation operates in other areas, as depicted in figure 6.

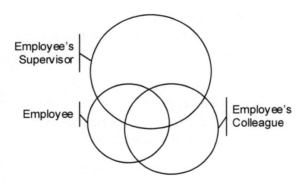

**Figure 6 – Shared Awareness Set model**

We can keep on adding more and more Awareness Sets to this picture for the organisation. But, as we extend the model, its representation becomes increasingly difficult. This is because, in all but the simplest organisations, the Awareness Sets have extremely complex overlaps.

Importantly though, notice that; although *how* the organisation operates is *dependent* on the *combined set*, it is extremely rare for any organisations, other than the smallest, to have a single stakeholder who has an overall understanding about:

- *all* of the operations carried out by the organisation

- the characteristics of *all* of its stakeholders and

- *their* interactions with the organisation's data

In fact, this is a significant problem, because ideally we need to operate with an understanding and knowledge based upon the 'big-picture' for the organisation.

## The Subject Matter Expert

To help mitigate these shortcomings, it is always worth seeking testimony from people who have an Awareness Set that is a super-set of many other stakeholders.

These individuals are experts in their respective fields, and of course, we know them as Subject Matter Experts (SMEs).

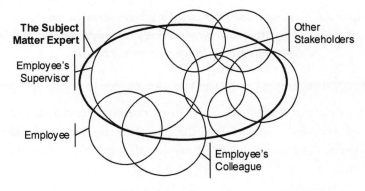

**Figure 7 – The Subject Matter Expert knowledge profile**

We can imagine the SME's Awareness Set as in shown in figure 7.

To aid the Data Architect in their quest for the elusive total organisational awareness, they must seek out and communicate effectively with SMEs.

## Engaging With SMEs

SMEs provide an excellent resource to help us understand the operational processes across the organisation. Importantly, they may also have a good understanding of the data usage of processes. Therefore, they can be extremely valuable to provide assistance when defining these.

Often though, engaging with SMEs can be much harder than you would imagine. Not only can finding the correct SME be difficult, but typically, these are the very individuals who have the least time to spare. This is because their expertise is usually in extremely high demand.

The Data Architect needs to establish a list of SMEs and create an effective working relationship with them. This activity should be a pre-cursor to working in any particular operational areas.

## Collective Loss of Memory

Severe retrenching and rehiring cycles can have a devastating effect on an organisation's collective knowledge. As a consequence, processes that provide continuity, can become inadequate and/or highly stressed[2].

---

*Principle 21*    ***A high churn rate of stakeholders in an organisation can severely damage its chances of immediate or longer term survival.***

---

A further negative impact of high churn rate may be that it also increases stress for retained stakeholders due to their increased workload. This can, in itself, further inhibit the transfer of knowledge and skills to new incumbents.

The damage to the collective knowledge and skills is illustrated by the following depleted Awareness Set diagram.

---

2    Business Continuity Management is a management discipline designed to help organisations plan and deploy strategies that will help them mitigate Process degradation caused by high churn rates.

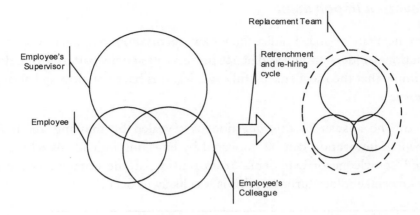

**Figure 8 – High churn rate Awareness Set atrophy**

Figure 8 indicates that the replacement team have much smaller individual Awareness Sets, and Awareness Set overlap, than their previous incarnation. Naturally this can cause significant negative impacts on operational outcomes.

## Process Resilience

Because of their comprehensive framework of process definitions, franchises are good examples of organisations that potentially have good resilience to high stakeholder churn rates.

This organisational resilience, forms the basis of principle 22.

> *Principle 22*    *The Organisations that are most likely to be resilient to a high churn rate of stakeholders, will have clearly documented, agreed and disseminated process definitions.*

Data Architects can contribute to this resilience, by ensuring that they create thorough documentation through formal artefacts and ensure effective dissemination of these artefacts.

## *Innovation Impairment*

Low churn rate of stakeholders allows an organisation to retain its collective operational understanding and hence preserve its activity patterns. But, does this imply that the most successful organisations have very low stakeholder turnover?

Part of the answer to this question, is revealed by thinking about the following; innovation can be imported by engaging individuals who have gained knowledge or experience from outside of the organisation. With very low stakeholder turnover, this is less likely to occur.

| | |
|---|---|
| *Principle 23* | *A low churn rate could have disastrous consequences for the longer term viability of an organisation, since it may leave the organisation potentially less able to adapt to changes in the environment in which it operates.* |

The Data Architect needs to act as an external consultant to an organisation, by being aware of and pioneering relevant innovations for it that are drawn from outside of its operations. This can make it better able to adapt to change, even where it has good stakeholder retention.

# Aligning an Organisation's Operations

In the previous sections, we considered organisational fitness and a way of modelling effort versus beneficial output. Although we can understand how these factors have a significant impact on an organisation's operations, they do not provide the whole picture.

A further critical part of an organisation's ability to succeed, is determined by the alignment of its individual stakeholders with the organisation. An extremely useful, yet simple analogy to model this is provided by the Domain Theory of magnetism.

This argues that in order for a material to become a magnet (i.e. provide an overall magnetic field), it must have a majority of its magnetic domains aligned.

In a magnetic material without an overall magnetic field, the magnetic domains' orientations are randomised, and therefore the effect of each is cancelled by the effect from its neighbours.

**Principle 24** *If the effects of the individual domains' are nullified by its neighbours, there is little or no overall effect.*

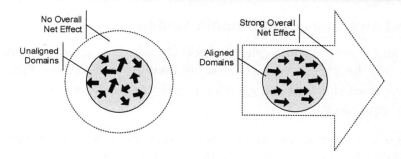

**Figure 9 – Aligning domains**

However, if the individual domains' magnetic orientations are aligned, the material exerts an overall net magnetic field, that is, the material acts as a magnet.

**Principle 25** *The better the alignment of individual domains, the stronger their overall effect is.*

This provides an extremely powerful visualisation of an organisation's effectiveness.

We can think of an organisation's individual stakeholders exhibiting the equivalents of these magnetic domains. Each domain represents a set of internalised goals, strategies, policies and guidelines.

If we were able to simplify these, and map them to those of the organisation, then we can imagine that we could measure the degree of their alignment. By analogy, the higher this degree of alignment, the more effective and organisation can become.

> **Principle 26** **An organisation whose stakeholders' internalised models and behaviours are well aligned with its overall strategies, is potentially able to be more far effective.**

## Combined Awareness and Domain Models

The preceding concepts and models support the idea that although two individuals may have a large intersection of their Awareness Sets, their judgements, values, opinions and agendas may diverge significantly in any of the overlapped areas!

In figure 10, we see a combined representation of how the behaviour domains of each stakeholder, may be different to those of other stakeholders.

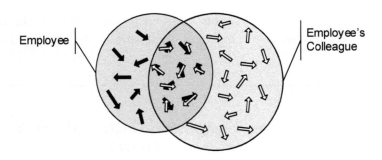

Employee

Employee's Colleague

**Figure 10 – Combined awareness and alignment model**

Figure 10 illustrates the well-known phenomenon of individual stakeholders working *against* each other.

The Data Architect needs to consider this concept of alignment when attempting to exert influence within an organisation. We all know that little can be achieved unless the involved stakeholders are 'all on the same page'.

To bring this about may take time. As a result, the Data Architect sometimes has to play a patient waiting game, until ideas that initially seemed radical, become everyone's perception of normal ways of thinking.

## Controlling an Organisation's Future

We have now established some of the fundamentals of data and its relationship with an organisation, as well as characteristics of stakeholders, including alignment.

Let's now describe the foundations for how an organisation can create data related frameworks and processes that will enable it to adapt to face its future.

This seems like an impossible task because surely the future cannot be known?

We will return to this question repeatedly in this book, because in fact a great deal *can* be predicted about an organisation's future and the book will describe some simple thought exercises that can be used to prepare the organisation for likely scenarios.

**One thing is absolutely for certain though - if an organisation ignores its future, it is unlikely to have one!**

In order to think about how to establish an effective framework, I want to use the simple model of Adaptive Control Systems.

A long time ago, I worked as an Aeronautical Engineer on a military aircraft that was then under development. The team I worked in was the Spin Prevention Team.

Fighter aircraft need to be extremely agile and able to change course very rapidly. As a result, they are barely stable[3]. This means that the pilot cannot actually safely control the aircraft without the aid of Control System software. The job of this software is to mediate the changes that impact the aircraft, not least of which are the pilot's commands!

One of the biggest problems, is where the pilot tries to make a manoeuvre that forces the aircraft to go into an irreversible condition, for example, certain types of spins. No matter what the pilot does from that point on,

---

3    This is analogous of the start-up phase of an organisation!

the aircraft cannot be made to return to a controllable condition.

If we view an aircraft as a complex system, the way this works is as follows; the Control System software compares an **idealised model** of the aircraft with the actual aircraft, using flight system data. Feedback loops use this comparison data to correct any adverse behaviour of the *actual* aircraft.

So, if the pilot tries to carry out a manoeuvre that would result in an irrecoverable state, the Control System compares the actual aircraft response with the idealised one, and mediates the pilot's input to be benign. This technique makes the actual aircraft behave in a way that is closer to its *idealised* model.

Simple eh?

We can apply this approach within the scope of our organisations and the schematic in figure 11 illustrates this simple feedback mediation.

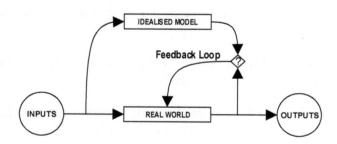

**Figure 11 – Idealised Model and feedback loops[4]**

If we abstract an organisation to a (very complex) system, then the same principles can be applied if:

1. An Idealised Model has been defined

2. Appropriate and accurate data can be collected about the organisation's operations and

3. There are effective feedback processes to adapt the organisation's operations

4    Comparing this with figure 3, we can see how the feedback loop mediates the inputs to become desired outputs.

So what do each of the three required elements represent in an organisation's equivalent Control System?

## The Idealised Model

To survive and thrive, organisations need to embrace a constant cycle of improvement. They must adopt this approach to make them better at what they do, and better at being able to adapt.

A critical part of the way that organisations need to assure their operational effectiveness, is by establishing Idealised Models. These models can then be compared with their actual operations, to identify any changes that need to be made to improve them.

The Idealised Model for an organisation, corresponds to its *defined* collective: goals, aims, strategies, policies, standards and guidelines.

To be effective though, these cannot simply be a collection of artefacts buried somewhere in document repositories, or on the organisation's intranet. They must have a *direct effect* on the organisation, through their *adoption* by its stakeholders.

| | |
|---|---|
| *Principle 27* | ***The Idealised Models for an organisation need to have a real impact on all of its day to day operations and the evolution of its strategies.*** |

Critically though, the Idealised Models must also have an in-built capacity to evolve over time!

| | |
|---|---|
| *Principle 28* | ***To remain relevant and effective into the future, any Idealised Models used within an organisation, must be able to evolve over time.*** |

This also implies that we must find ways to adapt the organisation's Idealised

Models as well as its operational activities.

But how?

## Collecting Accurate Data

The core rationale for Data Architecture is to improve the benefit to an organisation from its data. A significant part of this data must be to provide the organisation with an understanding of how; its operations *alter* the Real World, and equally importantly, how it *responds* to changes in the Real World.

What is now apparent is that a key part of all of the data flows is the data required within the feedback process illustrated in figure 11.

> **Principle 29**  *A critical part of all the data flows within an organisation, are those required to provide effective feedback into its Idealised Models.*

Data Architects need to consider this feedback loop in almost all of their activities. A common mistake made during deliveries is to focus purely on the immediate requirements.

Rarely, in the absence of Data Architectural influence, is account taken of the impact of specific implementations on the organisation's longer term and wider strategic direction.

If we think back to the aircraft example, there were two classes of data that could be used to analyse the real aircraft. These are the data obtained from the aircraft's

1.  Internal flight systems – e.g. height, ground speed, yaw and roll

2.  External environment – e.g. air density, wind speed and shear

Almost all organisations that use data to support their operations, collect and analyse the first class of data. Most are beginning to assess the potential benefits from the second.

For organisations, the second class of data relating to the Environment in which it operates, may not have been available to them in the past. However, as we shall see in the later chapter devoted to Big Data, it is becoming increasingly better *Known* and also increasingly *Shareable*.

## Feed-forward and Feedback Data Flows

When considering the contrast between what *is done* and what *needs to be done*, questions are immediately raised, such as:

- How does an organisation know whether it is a fit organisation or not?

- How does it adapt to change?

- If it is unfit, then what can it do to improve its fitness?

As we have seen, the answers to such questions are partly to do with collecting accurate and relevant data. Feedback data flows as shown in figure 11, will allow organisations to do more of what they *need* to do, and *reduce* or *remove* any wasted effort. But it is what an organisation *does* with this data that will determine how well it is positioned to face its future.

We will need to consider a comprehensive map of processes that will enable these capabilities. In the subsequent chapters we will describe exactly how an organisation's data-related Idealised Models should be designed and implemented.

# 2: Data Modelling

*How do we share the collective vision of our data's definitions and structures, across the organisation?*

In order to make sense of the world around us, humans invariably group things together that are alike, and create associations between them.

We *need* to do this, it is how we build internalised maps of our worlds.

But this idea applies equally to our organisations.

In their worlds, Clients do not exist in isolation[5]. They place Orders, consume Products/Services, and make Enquiries and Payments. In order for the organisation to function optimally, we need to agree and share these definitions between all the stakeholders. These definitions are the organisation's data Entities and their Relationships.

But how can we share the definitions of these data Entities, and the associations that exist between them, within our organisation's data world?

This is where Logical Data Models come into the picture – literally.

Logical Data Models create one of the most powerful tools in Data Architecture. They have a purpose to specify, communicate and facilitate agreement, on a common set of definitions of the data used throughout an organisation. These definitions are formed of the *meanings* and *patterns* of data.

Arguably, data models are now more important than ever. It is only with a full and agreed understanding of the 'What?', 'When?' and 'How?' of an organisation's data structures and flows, that we can contemplate plugging COTS products together, implementing in the Cloud, or reporting *across* the Enterprise system landscape.

For many organisations, a key outcome of adopting Big Data has been the newfound realisation of the importance of Logical Data Models. This

---

re-discovery has however, fundamentally altered the *way* that data models are viewed as providing support.

Whereas, in previous times they may have been restricted to being seen as an 'unwelcome' but necessary part of development, they are now being recognised for what they truly are; a definition of the operational lifeblood of an organisation.

As a result, in the last decade data models have made the transition from being ad-hoc and limited in scope, to becoming a central pillar of the Enterprise Architectural landscape.

This chapter does not intend to teach data modelling techniques. For these you may want to refer to the 'The Data Model Toolkit' book by the same author, or another of the readily available resources. What it will do though, is provide some simple practises that can be used to gain *more benefit* from the process of data modelling, with the added bonus of *reducing* the required effort.

## Logical Data Models

Many technologists will assert that data models are irrelevant because; 'we are using a schema-less database', or 'we define our data on the fly', or 'we are using Big Data'

But these viewpoints misunderstand the purpose and importance of the Logical Data Models.

Years ago the origin of data models lay in the need to specify data structures for system development, and even today, some people believe that this is still the extent of their scope.

Although the world has moved on a great deal since those days, and custom development is the exception now rather than the norm, data models remain crucially important for organisations in today's world. This is because they provide a detailed specification of the data that flows through an organisation's veins.

Without such data flows, most (certainly all the larger) organisations' operations are brought to a grinding halt *very quickly*. For evidence of this, just think of the enormous sums of money organisations spend on providing and verifying back-up and fail-over capability for so many of the world's systems.

Whether we are: selecting an appropriate COTS[6] product, or hooking bespoke systems together through Web Service calls, or feeding data into Consolidation Hubs, or Data Warehouses, we face the same fundamental questions:

- **What** is the **data**?
- **How** is it **defined** and **structured**?
- **When** is it **captured** and **modified**?
- **Where** are its **sources** and **destinations**?
- **Who** has **access** and **control** of which **parts** of it?

It is the Logical Data Models that allow us to record and agree definitions of the data. These definitions can be used as the basis of the answers to the preceding questions and for many others.

Indeed, they are now arguably more important than ever. Where they used to be isolated within each system development, all organisations are now beginning to appreciate the importance of their communication role at an Enterprise level.

---

*Principle 30*    ***Logical Data Models are fundamental to Data Architecture, and provide the basis to maximise the benefit to an organisation from its data.***

---

So that we can share an understanding of them, Geographical maps rely on relating landscape elements spatially with each other. In the same way, we need to link our data elements to each other to construct a shareable map of our data landscape. It is the ability to look at the same data map as other stakeholders, and *share* and *agree* the understanding of the data that makes them such powerful tools.

---

6    Commercial off the Shelf Products.

In other words, quite literally; the way that we see the data structures and patterns, is the same way that others in the organisation see them too.

> *Principle 31*  **Logical Data Models record, and make shareable, the <u>definitions</u> and <u>structures</u> of an organisation's data and hence document its meaning framework.**

Notice though that so far we have not mentioned any system applicability for the Logical Data Model.

It is critical to understand that the Logical Data Model must be defined using only Operational and Business understanding.

And as such, it must not reference any potential implementation specifics including technology.

> *Principle 32*  **Logical Data Models record the Operational and Business meanings of an organisation's data structures and patterns, and <u>must be technology agnostic</u>.**

## The Data Model Communication Tool

Data modelling is a key technique that allows organisations to define, communicate and agree the *meaning* of their data and the patterns that exist within it.

> *Principle 33*  **The only reason Logical Data Models exist is to <u>communicate</u> understanding and facilitate agreement on the data definitions and patterns.**

Once we understand that principle 33 describes the true purpose of data models, we realise that their *key feature needs to be clarity*.

With this in mind, let's consider the importance of the Logical Data Model as a communication tool.

## Data Model Syntax Mediation

We must always be mindful of the fact that Logical Data Models use symbolic representations. In chapter 1, we stated that communication is mediated by its dissemination mechanism and the characteristics of its audience.

Therefore, one of the key factors influencing the success of any data modelling is the symbolic language used, which can introduce mediation of understanding.

This symbolic language can have two key negative aspects to its interpretation that act:

1. as a communication barrier

2. to skew understanding

These aspects are described in more detail below.

### *Syntax Interpretation Barrier*

We tend to assume that data models *facilitate* communication of data patterns and definitions. What can sometimes be forgotten is that data models use a symbolic representation and that not every stakeholder will read them in the same way as you do!

| | |
|---|---|
| *Principle 34* | *If the data modelling syntax is not understood by the audience, then it will act as a barrier to, rather than an enabler of, communication.* |

Consider the example in figure 12.

**Figure 12 – "You See What I Mean?"**

Unless we understand the symbols, the message is lost!

### Syntax Interpretation Skews

The syntax of data models can also introduce constraints on the model definitions as stated in principle 35.

| | |
|---|---|
| **Principle 35** | *Adopting certain data modelling syntax definitions, or even modelling tools, can skew understanding because their different syntax frameworks can force different models to be created.* |

For example, several data modelling tools used widely across the globe, do not support Barker Notation. This prevents the use of Barker Notation for Arcs and Sub-types. As a result, all Logical Data Models developed using this tool, have to use different representations of such data patterns. This in turn, has an effect on the way that the data's understanding is communicated and may also skew potential implementation design transitions. Rarely, in my experience, are such factors a part of the modelling tool selection process.

# Splattergrams

I use the term Splattergram to describe data models that have been created ignoring their communication purpose, and whose layout fails to provide clarity.

> **Principle 36   Clarity of Logical Data Models is paramount in their role of communicating the shared understanding of data's meaning.**

Figure 13 is an example of a real Splattergram, a variation of which I am sure we have all seen at one time or another.

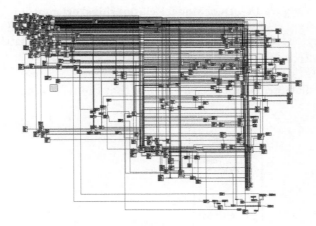

**Figure 13 – Example Splattergram**

The Data Architect must ensure that all data models are fit for purpose. At the very least, the data models should not contain crossing lines and have no overlapping!

In addition though, it is worth considering a methodical layout that can yield significant extra benefits from our models.

This is especially relevant to Normalised models including the:

- Logical Data Models

- Physical Data Models

It is strongly recommended that a layout is used that places the Many end of all Relationships towards the right or bottom for these model types.

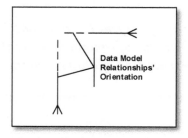

**Figure 14 – Data Model Relationships' orientation**

Once this style is adopted, the diagrams actually communicate much more information from the data model.

As an immediate consequence, we notice that the following characteristics are revealed.

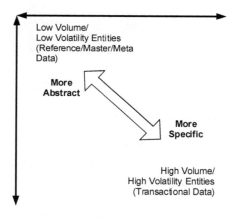

**Figure 15 – Data model patterns revealed by methodical layout**

At a glance, we suddenly have a lot more information, for instance:

- the high volume Entities and

- which data needs to be considered as context data

Once you take the effort required to lay out data models methodically, something really weird happens.

At some stage, small children learn to start reading rapidly, using pattern matching techniques, and stop reading words letter by letter. In the same way, you will notice that to gain an understanding of the model no longer requires you to trace your finger around it, mouthing the Entity and Relationship names! Instead, you will have the gist of the model at a glance, and begin to spot Rule Based and other structural patterns.

In other words, you will be able to start to assimilate and also quality assure models rapidly and in ways previously impossible!

Okay, this may sound a bit like a crazy money-back type of promotion, but I challenge you to try it!

## Data Model Longevity

Before we get into the detail of data modelling, here is a strange and maybe surprising thing to consider; think of some organisations and play back their operational data domains 20, 50 or even 100 years.

For many organisations, the fundamental Real World data relating to their operational inputs or outcomes, has not changed significantly over these timeframes.

> *Principle 37*     **Within an organisation's operational data scope, accurate Logical Data Models can remain true representations over extended periods of time[7].**

As an example, imagine car manufacturers a century ago; their contemporary Logical Data Model should be fairly consistent with one that could have been (hypothetically created) a hundred years ago!

---

7    The caveats for this Principle are that the model was originally not mechanistic and was *accurate*.

> ***Principle 38***     ***If Logical Data Models require updating significantly within a few years, then this may well be an indication that they weren't that well thought through originally.***

Data Architects should ensure that the Entities and data structures recorded in the Logical Data Models are an accurate representation of the organisation's data patterns. If this is well done, the models should have longevity baked into them.

A common cause of reduced longevity of Logical Data Models is that they contain mechanistic definitions. A further significant cause of changes in recent times, has been the advent of the global telecommunications network. This has enabled 'new' modes through which organisations can interact with their external world. As a result, the myriad of channels for communication and product/service distribution, has had a dramatic effect on many organisations' operations.

As a simple example, location based operations which used to only correspond to physical locations, could now be associated with more virtual locations, as exemplified by on-line purchasing.

In addition, because of the explosion of data creation and capture in the last few decades, the *Known* and *Shareable* domains of data have been radically extended. This aspect will be considered in more detail in the Big Data chapter later in this book.

## Building Logical Data Models

Okay, we now realise the importance of Logical Data Models, but how do we set about their construction?

Figure 16 illustrates the way that the overall data modelling processes[8] need to consume the characteristics of an organisation's (rather messy) Real World data, and define neat, well organised and agreed outputs from it.

---

8    For more background to developing Data Models please refer to the book by the same author - 'The Data Model Toolkit', ISBN: 978-1782224730.

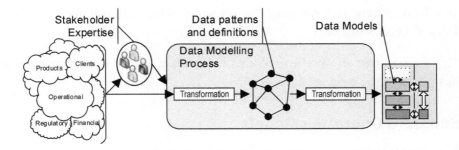

**Figure 16 – The data modelling process overview**

---

*Principle 39*    *Importantly, definitions need to be relevant to, and aligned with, the organisation for which they are developed.*

---

The alignment of the data's definitions with the organisation can only realistically be achieved, with the commitment and involvement of a number of key stakeholders in the organisation. This will ensure that the different operational viewpoints of our data combine to create consensus around its definitions.

## The Data Model Basis

Data models have to come from somewhere[9].

They must represent the definitions and structures of data that allow the organisation to operate optimally. Because of this, they must be based on what an organisation *does*, or maybe more importantly, what it *should be doing*.

---

*Principle 40*    *A __comprehensive__ understanding of an organisation's relationship with its data, can only be derived from the definitions of the data's __usage__ by the __activities__ it carries out.*

---

9   And I don't mean the Internet! ☺

But from where will we gain the understanding that will feed into the Logical Data Models?

Key sources that should be exploited if possible, are the activity models as described in the next section.

## Standard Operating Models

Many organisations attempt to define and standardise the way that they carry out their operations. This can produce major benefits for the organisation, including easier on-boarding of new staff, and providing consistency in the delivery of their products and services.

The way that they do this is by defining a Standard Operating Model[10] (SOM), which aims to provide a standardised blueprint of the way that an organisation should carry out its activities.

A well-defined SOM should also specify the way that data is used within its activity definitions[11]. This can sometimes be at a low level of detail. Thus, these models can be used as a comprehensive source to accelerate and validate, the construction of the Logical Data Models.

> *Principle 41*    ***A set of SOM definitions will (ideally) specify the data usage of the organisation's operations.***

Figure 17 shows how the data and related activity models, have Real World reflections.

---

10    Sometimes this concept is interchangeably referred to as Standard Operating Procedures (SOP). Also in this era of more rapid change organisations develop a steady stream of Target Operating Models.
11    Later in the book we will see how to use this technique in the form of our Data Governance process definitions.

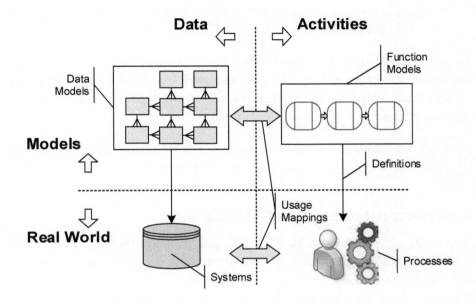

**Figure 17 – Models versus the Real World**

Any available SOM models, should form part of the source artefacts that are used to define the Logical Data Models. This is because, they can provide a well-defined catalogue of the activities that can act to; consume, capture, generate, modify and/or produce data for an organisation's operations.

> *Principle 42*  *Ideally, SOM definitions should be used as key resources to define the Logical Data Models, since they should define the interactions between an organisation's operations and its data.*

Although SOM models can be invaluable sources when defining the data required by an organisation, a degree of caution should always be applied to them. It can be dangerous to assume that these models accurately represent what is *really* carried out within the organisation because, for example:

- the initial analysis may have been flawed

- the organisation has 'moved on' since the definitions were captured

- people are remarkably adept at ignoring the way that they are told to do something!

In addition, it must be remembered that for data models to allow an organisation to thrive, they must be insulated from poorly implemented, or redundant activities, and instead be based upon *idealised* definitions of these activities.

How an organisation can implement data related changes to improve its operations, is examined in a lot more detail in later chapters of this book.

## Cost/Benefit of Logical Data Models

When defining data models, I have found that the technique generally follows the 80/20 rule. That is, 80% of the model can be defined with about 20% of the overall effort. The '80% of the model definition' refers to the majority of the Entities, their headline Attributes and their Relationships being correctly modelled.

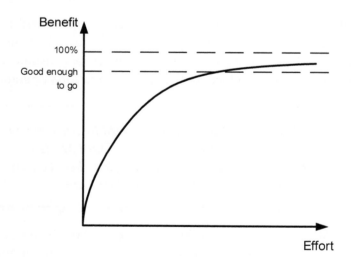

**Figure 18 – Data modelling effort to benefit plateau**

The chart in figure 18 illustrates a typical effort versus benefit plateau of data modelling[12].

---

12    I'm afraid that a key point it also illustrates, is that data models will *never* be a 100% perfect representation of the real world.

Once the benefit plateau is reached, expending more effort, may not be sufficiently beneficial to the organisation to be justified. This is the point where, before expending any further development of the model, the 'Do we care?'[13] challenge should be applied!

When applying this challenge, we must always bear in mind that the Logical Data Models will *never* be *completed*. They will need to evolve in step with changes in the organisation, even if for no other reason.

## Data Model Accuracy

Data models must represent our organisation's interpretation of the Real World. If they do this accurately, then we should be able to answer any hypothetical questions from them that we could ask of the Real World that they represent.

For example:

'What is the average lead time by Product and Region from Payment to Fulfilment?'

---

*Principle 43*    ***For the data area it covers, a good data model should allow you to answer <u>any</u> hypothetical question that could possibly be posed of the Real World.***

---

The difficulty in determining a data model's accuracy can lead to a stalling in the modelling process. Therefore, let's turn our attention to the *process* of data modelling.

## 'Tweakening' Data Models

Data model *accuracy* is of course a phantom. The trick is to recognise that you have reached the 'good enough' level of its development. But how do you know when you have reached this point?

---

13    This challenge allows us to decide whether, sufficient *benefit* will be derived by any *extra effort*, to justify it being expended.

You may want to consider the following tell-tale signs, for example, when you are beginning to:

- tweak the model's micro structures repeatedly

- fiddle endlessly with datatype precisions

- repeatedly wait for feedback on clarifying a few more attribute's definitions with SMEs

If a couple of these sorts of signs characterise the current point in the modelling process, then consider either:

- having a break to come back to it afresh, or

- moving on to other activities that are more productive

## Data Model Confidence Levels

I have always noticed something about my experience of data modelling, which is characterised by the chart in figure 19.

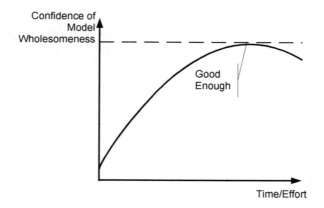

**Figure 19 – Data model wholesomeness confidence**

When starting a data model, my confidence that I have an accurate and complete representation is understandably low. As time goes on, I begin to feel much more confident. Many times I have felt that it is good enough, and I have learned to stop at that point and come back to it the next day or after the weekend.

Sometimes however, revisiting it makes me realise that actually:

- there are structural problems with it, or:

- it is over engineered in certain areas, or

- it is totally inadequate in certain areas

However, the more time I devote to it, the more my disquiet about it grows and I start to play endless new scenarios to test the models' representation against.

This is *almost* *good* *behaviour*. But there needs to be a point where you recognise that, actually more time and effort is *decreasing* your confidence, whilst quite possibly *not* improving the accuracy that you strive for.

When you recognise this set of behaviours, it should tell you that you definitely need to stop fiddling, twiddling and fine-tuning the model! In other words, recognise the point when the data model *is good enough*.

Of course, this is not to say that it is finished or static. Processes will need to be defined that will allow the model to continue evolving to become more accurate and remain relevant to the organisation.

We'll describe how these can be practically integrated with your organisation's delivery processes later in the book.

## Data Model Completeness

Assuming that a data model is sufficiently accurate to ensure its longevity, there are two main questions that need to be answered in order to determine whether a data model is *complete*, these are:

1. Does the model cover the required scope?

2. Is it sufficiently detailed?

Let's look at these in more detail in the following sections.

## Does the data model cover the required scope?

How do you know whether the entire required data scope of the data model is covered?

A few simple techniques that can be used to double check this are described below.

## Functional Support Matrix

A high-level Logical Data Model can be used to produce a high-level Function to Entity matrix. This can be used as a tool to provide a sanity check ensuring sufficient coverage by the model. Where this can be particularly useful, is for verifying very large and/or complex models. This technique's simplified representation, prevents the detail from getting in the way of the overall, high-level quality assurance of the model's completeness.

## Testing the Scope Boundary

In part, completeness refers to the data scope boundary. Therefore, to ascertain whether a data model is complete, start to ask some hypothetical questions of the model at the *boundaries* of its scope.

## Is It Future-proofed?

Earlier we looked at how, if sufficiently accurate, data models can have longevity measured in decades. Another way of challenging the model's completeness is to look at how it would accommodate future deviations from the present. Are the structures sufficiently flexible to provide extensible future-proofing, for example?

> *Principle 44*  *A simple trick to check temporal resilience of your Logical Data Model, is to change the tense of your probing from 'Is this correct?' to 'Will this always be correct?'*

In chapter 1, we discussed the importance of removing mechanisms from our definitions. Carrying out a simple check of any mechanistic aspects of a model, can also assist in improving its longevity. This has a positive impact by making its temporal definition more 'complete'.

## *Lifecycle Structures*

A further set of challenges should be made to ensure that the data lifecycles are adequately covered by the model. Here, checks should be made to ensure that the data structures can support the data patterns that need to be captured over time. These patterns should support the Entity's' creation, modification and ultimate demise as a bare minimum. A good example of this is the process of Client on-boarding, where the various phases and the data captured during each, is often complex.

## *Check Reporting Requirements*

To provide an additional cross reference, you may also want to look at reporting, or other documented requirements, to check that the necessary supporting data structures exist.

Don't forget though, that any *specified* requirements should only be used as *clues* to the *full set* of potential data requirements. If the requirements change next week, would you need to change your model?

## Is The Model Sufficiently Detailed?

Correct scoping is a key part of the assurance of a model's completeness, but so is assuring that it's sufficiently complex.

Here we can make use of a principle nicely encapsulated by the Albert Einstein quote

**'A scientific theory should be as simple as possible, but no simpler.'**

Let's appropriate this quote, for a way of looking at the process of data modelling, as defined in principle 45.

---

*Principle 45*    *Data Models should be as simple as possible, but no simpler.*

---

Figure 20 illustrates this idea.

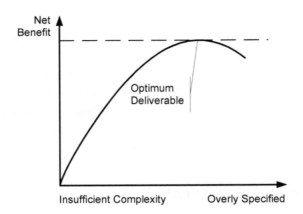

**Figure 20 – Optimum Data Model**

To check for the optimal simplicity of models, the following techniques can prove useful.

## Group Review to Validate

Checking a data model for its wholesomeness is a very difficult activity. In my experience, the best way to validate a model is to review it with other people.

Walking them through your data model will test *your* understanding, as much as whether the participants actually agree with what you have done. Also, consider that their *lack* of understanding of the subject area, may actually be a benefit! This is because their lack of familiarity makes them ideally qualified to challenge a lot of the assumptions that you have unconsciously made in your evolution of the model.

## Reverse Engineering

You may also want to consider Reverse Engineering an existing Physical Data Model, or implemented system structures to act as *sanity checks*. In other words, 'Have we thought of everything or is there anything we've missed?' style interrogations.

A word of warning here though. There is a perception that Logical Data Models can simply be constructed from using earlier physical models and/

or data interface specifications, using a Reverse Engineering approach.

Whilst this approach does have some merit, extreme caution should be exercised with this technique.

> **Principle 46**   **_Blindly_ Reverse Engineering system definitions to form the basis of new models, runs a significant risk of constraining an organisation's _future_ to the _mistakes_ of its _past!_** [14]

Where this approach can be useful, is to speed up the process of constructing large models, since the landscape of the model can be put together quickly.

But of course, bear in mind that there still remains the arduous task of fleshing out this model. The process of challenging the detail of these large models, may actually be slower than green-field thinking. This can be especially true where significant structural problems with the model are unearthed, *after* you have spent a lot of effort refining the definitions at a detailed level!

### Do We Care?

If you have ever defined data models, I am sure you will have had the experience when you suddenly realise that parts of the model are actually a lot more complex than you had previously thought. This can happen, for instance, due to newly discovered information about data lifecycles, or much more complex inter-relationships between the Entities than originally believed.

These discoveries can lead you to want to amend your model with ever more complexity in a bid to more accurately represent the Real World. But in fact, whether this should be done needs to be challenged by the 'Do we care?' test. An initial question that might arise from the application of this principle is, 'How often are these complex patterns encountered?'

Even if they occur quite frequently, there is a follow-on question that is 'How much would it *really compromise* the organisation if we couldn't

---

14   More detail is provided in the 'Architectural Agility' chapter.

accurately represent these scenarios?'

In other words, is the extra complexity justified? Consider too that increasing the complexity of the model may make it more difficult for anyone else to understand it, hence diminishing the model's communication effectiveness.

Also, we can't ignore that the evaluation of this challenge should take into account that any resulting additional *implementation* complexity may well incur:

- higher development and testing costs

- ultimately more complexity for users

## Typey Type Type Data Modelling

I remember very well the day when a Development DBA came over to my desk and exclaimed 'We're not having any of that Typey Type Type stuff in *my* Database!' Having delivered his declaration of prohibition, he spun on his heel and stomped off back to his workstation.

One of the most rewarding experiences for me as a Data Architect, was to witness the total transformation of this individual, as he started to appreciate the power of abstracting and using data structures and meta-data as:

1. defence against Software Engineers and

2. defence against dirty data and

3. providing rigorous development frameworks

After some months of us working together, he began to champion the approach and soon began to chastise those guilty of not modelling *correctly*; that is, of *not* using a Typey Type Type technique!

So what is Typey Type Type? Why can there be hostility to it, and what benefits can make it worth considering?

## Abstraction

We learned at the beginning of this book that data provides a way of describing and measuring what is happening in the Real World. To understand it, though, requires an agreed framework of definitions about the *meaning* of the data. Let's now examine the role of abstraction in this framework of definitions.

Abstraction is an extremely powerful tool that allows us to discern patterns by stripping away specificity.

| | |
|---|---|
| *Principle 47* | *The process of abstraction strips away any specific or mechanistic interpretations, revealing the essence of the data's meaning.* |

## Abstracting Names

One simple aspect of abstraction which is often overlooked, is that of abstracting the names of Entities, Attributes and Relationships.

Often the initial choice of names reflects the way things are currently carried out, and therefore can be highly mechanistic. This can arise as a consequence of using Process definitions, instead of abstracted Functions, as the source of our understanding.

The Data Architect needs to question the basis of the names used in data models and, wherever possible, abstract them. This will result in them being more resilient to future operational changes. Partly this can be done by simply removing any mechanistic references from them. So as a simple example, instead of naming an Attribute 'Is **Email** Sent', we should instead use 'Is **Communication** Sent'.

| | |
|---|---|
| *Principle 48* | *Removing <u>any</u> mechanistic or restrictive references from names used in data models, acts to improve their future-proof qualities.* |

## *Abstracting Domains*

By abstracting (typing) the Attribute values for an Entity into Domains, we begin to understand something about the Entity at a higher level. That is, there is something about the Entity that has significance and is defined at a more abstract level than the Entity instances themselves.

---

**Principle 49**   ***Abstraction provides a way of grouping definitions and meanings that exist at a level <u>above</u> the individual instances of data.***

---

These abstracted types themselves, can sometimes be further grouped or typified and also have their own extensive Attribution and Relationships with other Entities.

These levels of abstracted context are commonly referred to as Reference Data or meta-data. They tell us something about the data which itself has *meaning*. Essentially these form the context of the meaning framework we described in the first chapter.

We all know that the process of abstraction to higher levels can be carried out repeatedly, until ultimately, all discernible meaning is lost from a data model. Even at lower levels of abstraction, this important technique can provide a *barrier* to understanding. This is one reason why Typey Type Typing can sometimes get a bad reputation.

The Data Architect may need to consider how to mitigate a disadvantage of Typey Type Typing modelling, whereby it can result in the meaning of the model become obscured.

# Rule Based Modelling Technique

Rule Based Modelling is an approach to modelling that explicitly uses the Typey Type Type abstracted data structures, to constrain patterns of data.

Notice though that through the process of abstraction, the definitions and *understanding* of the data patterns, have been *enshrined* in the Reference or meta-data.

> **Principle 50** *The core concept of Rule Based Modelling is that the data structures representing the Typing of Entities, can be used to define <u>rules</u> that govern the <u>data's patterns</u> and <u>behaviour</u>.*

At its very simplest, we can think about this technique being used to ensure that data instances or transactions are constrained by Reference Data Domains. However, we can extend this idea to create far more complex structures that specify more sophisticated data rules, and even complex behavioural aspects of the data.

### Simple Rule Base Modelling example

Let's find out about the Rule Based Modelling technique, using the following very simple example.

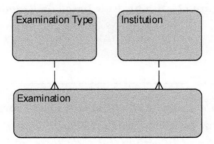

**Figure 21 – Simple data model fragment**

This model looks fine at first glance; an Examination instance is constrained to have taken place at a single Institution and is also of a particular Examination Type.

Notice though, that what is not constrained here is the *set* of Examination Types that it is *possible* to hold at any specific Institution. This allows the data to indicate that a degree examination took place at a toddler's kindergarten! Of course this *could* be totally valid, but the point here is that the model doesn't offer any defence against invalid data, by constraining the valid Examination Types for each Institution.

The model in figure 22, constrains the Examination Type of the Examination to be one of the possible Types that are offered at the Institution. By introducing this Rule Based Modelling Entity, we are able to constrain the Examination instance data, by using the Reference Data defined in the Rule Based data structures.

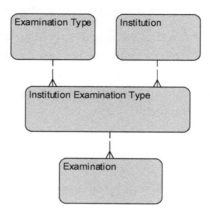

**Figure 22 – Simple Rule Based data model**[15]

Notice something important about this simple change that is described by principle 51.

| | |
|---|---|
| ***Principle 51*** | ***Rule Based data structures can store rules about data patterns that otherwise would need to be defined in either the code-base, or using some other mechanism!*** |

## *More Sophisticated Rule Based Modelling*

Imagine that we need to represent a simple Workflow. Figure 23 provides a typical example of a slightly more complex Rule Based Modelling structure.

---

15   Note that this Model asks the question, 'Is the set of Examination Types offered by each Institution *Shareable*?', in other words, 'How could we construct such a set and keep it current?' It may be, of course, that we can't!

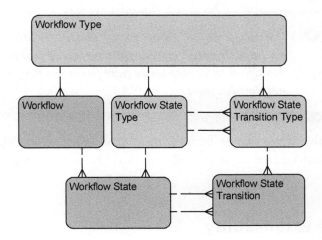

**Figure 23 – Basic workflow Rule Based data model**

This model provides the rules governing the transitions from one Workflow State to another[16]. This structure can be used to define the behaviour of data patterns and flows that can be used to control the code-base. This boosts organisational agility by:

1. Simplifying the initial code-base delivery

2. Enabling functionality modifications by *meta-data updates*

Even with these simple examples, we can see the immediate benefits. But why not think about extending this principle into more complex models?

This is where Rule Based Modelling really starts to deliver significant tangible benefits.

## Future-proofing Data Models

We typically use terms such as *extensible* or *flexible* when describing systems that are future-proofed. The basis for most of the functionality that characterises such systems is, of course, the data models that underpin them.

---

16 This schematic is a fragment of the larger model because here I just want us to clearly focus on the Rule Based State Transition part of the model.

> **Principle 52**   *'Future-proofed' refers to the characteristic of an implemented system that means it can be modified to incorporate new functionality with negligible effort.*

This means that if we want to increase the overall agility of an organisation, a key area to concentrate on, is embodying these characteristics within its data models.

## Attribute Extensibility

We have already described the benefits from using abstraction to ensure longevity, but there are other simple modelling techniques that you can use to make your models much more resilient to change. Incorporating data-driven structures provides extensibility features into the models. In the context of an organisation's data landscape, extensibility refers to the ability to accommodate new data patterns without significant effort or expense.

The expensive and slow part of many system deliveries and maintenance, is the development effort. However, a lot of value can be provided for your organisation, by incorporating extensibility capability into its data structures. If these become used as the basis for implementations, then they will take their inherent extensibility into the system landscape.

Therefore, if we think about it for a moment, extensibility is also a key factor of organisational agility.

> **Principle 53**   *Providing Extensible structures in Logical Data Models can increase organisational agility from their delivery into the system landscape.*

Even though such implementation considerations should not *drive* the Logical Data Models, we would be very wise to incorporate future-proofed qualities into them wherever possible.

What will vary over time are the data patterns that these implemented data models contain. These data pattern changes will need to be accommodated over short timeframes. For example, consider Anti-Money Laundering (AML) and Know Your Customer (KYC) implementations, where this requirement is prominent.

Within these areas, although we are able to define today's data requirements, new ones will constantly arise. We need to make our data models resilient to such changes. And we also need to consider how we are able to share this variable data across the system landscape - *without requiring additional development!*

The benefit of making extensibility part of the data models for implementations, is that the systems can use meta-data changes, to extend or modify their functionality. This provides a much more rapid response than, for example, requiring Software Engineers to make changes to the code-base. As a result, the system related savings and step changes in organisational agility can be dramatic.

The benefit is wider than this though.

What it means is that the data models also have longevity baked into them. Earlier we said that car manufacturers' data models created 50 years ago should be immune to the manufacturing and technological advances made since then. This can only be true if the *patterns of data capture* could have adapted over the decades.

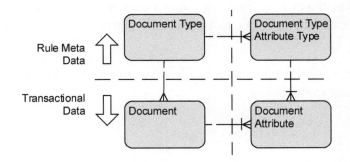

**Figure 24 – Extensible Rule Based data model**

Figure 24 shows a very simple *unchanging structure* that is able to accommodate changes to the structured data requirements for a Document over time.

This abstracted pattern can also be adopted for other extensible areas such as 'localised' attribution support.

# GLocalisation

GLocalisation is the term I use to describe the need for organisations to simultaneously support the Global and the Localised data requirements. Local language support is an obvious example for Localisation, but actually, the same concept has far more widespread applicability.

The Localisation could be for Product features, for example, or any data that does not have Enterprise scope.

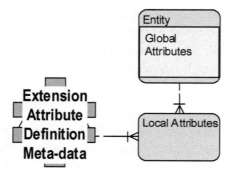

**Figure 25 – GLocalised Logical Data Model pattern**

Figure 25 illustrates a generalised pattern that uses concrete structures allowing Localised Attributes to be defined, captured and modified over time.

We shall return to this concept to see how we can build it into our system landscape later in the book.

# 3: Enterprise Data Models

*It is more critical than ever for our organisations to leverage the definitions of their data in order to survive and thrive.*

So far, we have described the importance of agreeing our data's definitions across the organisation. The pre-eminent tools to support this goal, are the Logical Data Models. But, by themselves, these cannot achieve all of the required transformations.

However, to enable the Logical Data Model to achieve these aims, is a wider family of data models called the Enterprise Data Models. Together, these can deliver an enormously positive impact to an organisation. They do this by establishing the comprehensive foundations for the organisation's shared understanding of its data. Their primary focus should be to provide points of reference through which the organisation, its stakeholders and the implemented systems, can be aligned.

This chapter considers the types of data models and associated artefacts that should be thought of as the Enterprise Data Models. Some of these models have a high degree of re-use within an organisation. Some form the basis of *all* of the other data models.

This chapter describes the way that together, the models form a coherent framework of data definitions, and reveals their individual purposes and inter-relationships.

## The Enterprise Data Model Family

In chapter 1, we learned that to maximise the benefit an organisation can derive from its data, we need to share its agreed meaning across the organisation. In the previous chapter we also discovered that the Logical Data Models are absolutely critical for sharing and agreeing this meaning across the organisation. But, by themselves, they cannot achieve the overarching need to share these definitions.

To assist them is a wider family of related models that provide the comprehensive foundation for sharing this agreed meaning.

This wider family is known as the Enterprise Data Models.

***Principle 54***     ***The Enterprise Data Models have a critical role to play in defining, communicating and agreeing data's <u>meaning</u> across an organisation.***

If these models provide the *medium* for communication, then it must be the *universally agreed meaning* of the data that forms the *content* of *what* they communicate.

This is encapsulated in principle 55.

***Principle 55***     ***The Enterprise Data Models must be based upon the firm foundations of the organisation's <u>shared and agreed understanding of its data</u>.***

Let's consider the different members of this family, and learn the characteristics of each.

At their core, the Enterprise Data Models comprise the following:

- Conceptual Data Models
- Logical Data Models
- Physical Data Models
- Canonical Models

We'll describe each of these, their individual characteristics and inter-relationships in the following sections.

## Conceptual Data Models

Although Logical Data Models are the definition hub of the Enterprise Data Models, they are based on an underlying source of definitions. These models are known as the Conceptual Data Models.

The Conceptual Data Model is a *very simple* high-level Entity data model. Its definitions of the high-level Entities must be framed in terms of the Business and Operational understanding of the data. This model *may* also specify their Relationships and contain a few headline Attributes, but these are not mandatory. Any Relationships would be no more than simple linkages, rather than rigorous definitions.

Within the realm of delivery, these models are typically used to define the data scope to confirm it with all stakeholders, particularly in the early stages.

They are typically considered and defined as a single high-level model; these should contain no more than 15 Entities. But in larger, more complex organisations, a group of Conceptual Subject Area Data Models may also sometimes be useful.

These two different levels are described in the following sections.

### Enterprise Conceptual Data Models

At the Enterprise level, Conceptual Data Models contain *all* of the organisation's high-level Enterprise Entities. At this level, for example, they might contain a dozen Entities including, for example: Party, Product, Legal Agreement and Payment.

---

**Principle 56**    *The primary purpose of Enterprise Conceptual Data Models, is to clearly communicate high-level Entities, and their meaning across the organisation.*

---

### Conceptual Model Subject Areas

For larger, complex organisations, a single Enterprise Conceptual Data Model is too simple to be useful.

In these cases, it needs to be broken into multiple more functionally focussed areas, such as:

- Product

- Finance

- Marketing

Each of these Conceptual Model Subject Areas would contain perhaps a dozen Entities that are relevant to a part of the organisation's operations. This allows the stakeholders to focus better on the definitions that they are more concerned and familiar with.

# Logical Data Models

Logical Data Models are more detailed, and fully normalised[17] models and should be derived from the Conceptual Data Model/s.

The primary reasons for defining Logical Data Models for an organisation is to define its data's:

- Scope

- Definitions

- Data Structures

All of the definitions must be created with Business and Operational understanding and framed in terms that these key stakeholders are familiar with.

By evolving them from the Conceptual Models, the coherence across these two important levels is assured.

---

*Principle 57*    *The Enterprise Conceptual Data Model must form the basis upon which the Enterprise Logical Data Models are developed.*

---

Figure 26 illustrates the development of the Logical Data Models using the Conceptual Data Model/s as their foundation.

---

17    Third Normal Form is typically the level of Normalisation used for these.

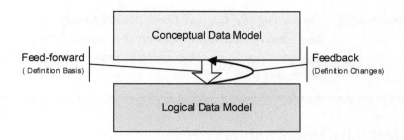

**Figure 26 – Logical Data Models' dependency on the Conceptual Data Model**

The key feature of this schematic is the feed-forward arrow. This indicates the inheritance of the definitions of the high-level Entities. It is the flow of these definitions that will ensure the initial coherence between these two levels of data models.

In the previous chapter, we discovered that the Logical Data Models will constantly need to evolve and will never be 'finished'. Figure 26 indicates that there are feedback flows that communicate any discoveries gained from subsequent detailed work on the Logical Data Models. This feedback is critical, and can arise as new understanding is revealed by more detailed discovery and decision making activities.

Later in the book, we will also see how the feedback can arise from the delivery processes, and how this is channelled back through dedicated processes.

## Logical Data Model Delivery Approach

It may not be feasible to complete large complex Logical Data Models in a single concerted effort. We need to make them more achievable by carving the effort up into smaller bite-sized chunks. These chunks are called Subject Areas, and are discussed in the next section.

Note that this approach allows us to work to a detailed level in one Subject Area, whilst leaving other areas at the Conceptual stage. Because of the traceability back to the Conceptual Model, we can do this and be confident of not compromising the overall model *coherence*.

> **Principle 58** **By basing the Logical Data Model firmly on the Conceptual Data Model, it is possible to _independently_ develop specific areas to much more detail.**

## Logical Data Model Subject Areas

To make their development and assimilation more manageable, we can chunk-up the overall Logical Data Model, into individual Subject Areas.

But how do we decide what constitutes a Subject Area?

It makes sense to guide the Subject Areas using the high-level Entities in the Conceptual Data Model. Each Subject Area would typically cover only one or two of the Conceptual Data Model high-level Entities, for example, Party, Payment or Product.

By basing the Subject Areas on the Conceptual Data Model Entities, the feed-forward flow of meaning can be assured. In other words, all of the high-level Entities have been normalised into their corresponding low-level Entities, in the Logical Data Model.

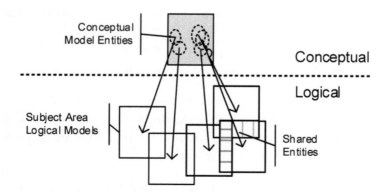

**Figure 27 – Developing Subject Areas of Logical Data Models**

Figure 27 illustrates how the Conceptual Data Models can be used as the basis to derive the more complex, lower level Logical Data Model Subject Areas.

> **Principle 59**   *Each of the Subject Areas in the Logical Data Models, can be based on one (or two) of the Entities from the Conceptual Data Model.*

Notice the Shared Entities in figure 27.

What we mean by Shared Entities, are those Entities that occur in more than one Logical Data Model Subject Area. The inclusion of these, ensures that the Subject Area models link together, and therefore guarantee coherence across the entire set of the Logical Data Model Subject Areas.

For example, a Party Role will typically appear in many of the Subject Area models, and thus provides the linchpin that bridges across these individual areas.

## The pre-eminence of the Logical Data Model

The Logical Data Model should be seen as the *foundational* data definition and structural model on which the others need to be based. The definitions it contains, need to be represented in other artefacts to aid their dissemination. The following can be considered common additional Enterprise Data Models:

1.   Data at Rest - Physical Data Models

2.   Data at Flow - Canonical Models

3.   Data Lexicons

## Data at Rest - Physical Data Models

Although custom development is not the norm any longer, we need to consider that *sometimes* we will still be using our Logical Data Models to produce a physical representation. Once they have reached the good enough to go stage, it is possible to progress their development into the physical word.

The physicalisation design process may well need to compromise the

Logical Data Model with all sorts of constraints. Some of these will be imposed by technologies, or other design factors, such as reporting and auditing requirements.

> **Principle 60**  *The process of creating Physical Data Models from Logical Data Models, is about transforming their implementation-agnostic representation, to a technology dependent representation.*

There are two classes of Physical Data Models:

1. Normalised Physical Data Models

2. De-normalised Physical Data Models

These are described in a little more detail below.

## Normalised Physical Data Models

When developing normalised Physical Data Models, it is critical to remember that *any* divergence of them from the normalised Logical Data Model, may cause a corresponding divergence from the *understanding* and *meaning* that was defined and agreed *within* the Logical Data Model[18].

As a simple example of this, consider the data structure rule that; 'each Client can hold more than one Account' and that 'each Account can be held by more than one Client'. These data rules need to be defined in the Logical Data Model, but must also be reflected in any dependent Physical Data Model.

> **Principle 61**  *Normalised Physical Data Models should be developed minimising any deviation of the data's meaning from that defined within the corresponding Logical Data Model.*

---

18    Whilst the above is true, all sorts of constraints may dictate that a degree of divergence is the *best* option available at the time.

By comparison with the Enterprise Logical Data Model, the normalised physical representation may potentially lose; Entities, Attributes and Relationships, that are not required for a specific implementation. It may also gain elements including, for example, the addition of; access control, auditing, or scheduling structures.

Also, bear in mind that creating these models at an Enterprise level, is only justified, where there are anticipated to be many repeated implementations within a *single* technology, for example, Oracle, Mongo DB or Teradata.

## De-normalised and Dimensional Physical Data Models

The design decisions for de-normalising a normalised model may be complex and arise for many reasons including reporting simplification, or performance gains.

Typically however, when considering de-normalised models, some people immediately think of standard Star, or Snowflake Dimensional modelling styles, as if these are the only structures that could be used.

Whilst useful, styles specified by Dimensional modelling luminaries, should only be used as sanity checks for models that the organisation evolves.

---

*Principle 62*    *Any Enterprise de-normalised data models, need to represent data in a way that fits an organisation's needs.*

---

When evolving these models, their relationship to the Conceptual and High-level Logical Data Models cannot be ignored.

In addition, what is paramount, is that any de-normalisations must be *consistent* with the structural definitions defined in the normalised Logical Data Model.

> ***Principle 63*** ***De-normalised models must be coherent with,***
> ***and have clear, traceable dependencies, on the***
> ***definitions and structures defined in the Logical***
> ***Data Model.***

For example, any collapsed hierarchies, or aggregated Attributes in a de-normalised model, must be consistent with their related normalised elements. We will return to this theme in the 'Agile Data Flows' chapter.

## Cycle of Physical Data Model Development

Consider the circle of development of data models and data flows represented in figure 28. This schematic suggests that the de-normalised models can be considered as providing at least a partial reversal of the normalisation processes that initially produced the Logical and Physical Data Models.

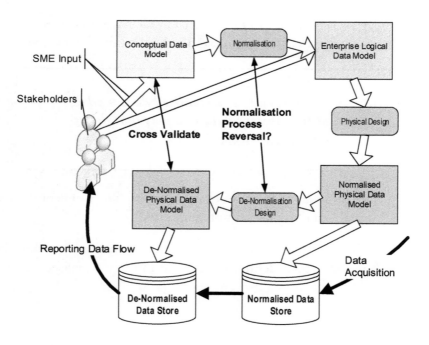

**Figure 28 – The cycle of data model development**

In this respect, data sourced from the implemented de-normalised data structures, is effectively brought back with a representation that is familiar to the stakeholders. It was (hopefully), this exact same stakeholder understanding that formed the basis of the Conceptual and Logical Normalised Models in the first place.

This cycle illustrates the criticality of the abstract Conceptual and Logical Data Models, in defining the data structures and patterns that provide the rigour to make the de-normalised data models fit for purpose.

## Data at Flow – Interface Models

Increasingly, the challenges that organisations face are not caused by custom Data at Rest development. Instead, they frequently arise from the requirement to plug Cloud-based solutions together to form the organisation's system backbone.

As a result, the Data at Rest definitions are not nearly as important as those of Data at Flow. But surely, although our data models are good at describing physical data structures, we won't be able to use them to define our interface definitions?

Well, in fact we can - and we *must*.

Wherever data *flows* across the organisation's system landscape, the Logical Data Models *must* retain their authority.

---

**Principle 64**  *To ensure optimal flows of data across our organisation's system landscape, the Logical Data Models __must__ be used to conform the Data at Flow definitions.*

---

In fact, they have become the crucial foundation of data's definitions and structures for the interfaces in a Loosely Coupled system landscape.

## Canonical Models

The Canonical Model describes the definition and structure of the data elements that flow across the organisation's system landscape. They are crucial to provide the basis on which to validate the specifications of interfaces, for example, APIs.

> **Principle 65** *High-level interface models must be formed using the Logical Data Models as their basis.*

The Canonical Models *must* be formed using the Conceptual and Logical Data Models as their basis, and not the Physical Data Models. This is because, the latter will almost certainly have been compromised as a part of the design process.

> **Principle 66** *Canonical Data Models must be used to define and conform the language of data transfer that is used across the organisation.*

As a result of using this approach, we can ensure that all our interfaces will 'play nicely together'. We will return to the development of the Enterprise Canonical Models as a *pre-requisite* for the exchange of data between systems in the 'The Seven Principles Of Data' chapter.

## Data Model Inter-relationships

Since the Enterprise Data Models are formed using the Conceptual and Logical Data Models as their foundation, there are naturally very strong inter-relationships between them all.

> **Principle 67** *At their very core, the Enterprise Data Models are absolutely dependent on their shared data meanings and patterns.*

Figure 29 illustrates the relationships between the various Enterprise Data Models.

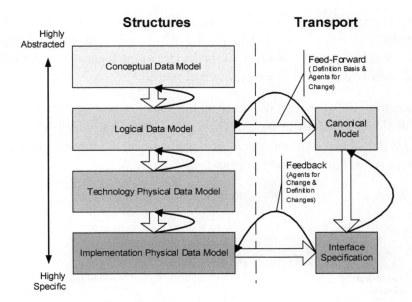

**Figure 29 – The Enterprise Data Model inter-relationships**

The most abstract are Conceptual Data Models, and the most specific are those models developed for specific Physical Data Model implementations.

## Feed-forward Degree of Re-use

The feed-forward changes, represent the flow of definitions from the highest level of abstraction, to the lowest. This indicates that the definitions of the lower level models are derived from, and therefore dependent on, the corresponding definitions held at a higher level.

| | |
|---|---|
| *Principle 68* | *The data's definitions and structures must be inherited from the most abstract models to the most specific.* |

The structures and attribution of the abstract Enterprise Data Models, will have the highest degree of re-use across the organisation. The implementation specific models, will obviously have the lowest degree of re-use, and quite possibly, none at all.

In larger organisations, it may make sense to develop and maintain Enterprise *Technology* Physical Data Models. These will contain standardised technological transformations that make them immediately usable for specific implementations across the organisation.

For example, imagine that we want to have an Oracle Operational Data Store deployed in the three regions of; the Americas, Asia and EMEA. The Oracle Physical Data Model, would be defined once, but implemented, and therefore re-used, in the three regions.

The schematic in figure 30 illustrates this concept.

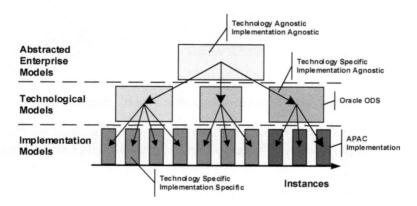

**Figure 30 – The Enterprise Data Models' degree of re-use**

## Feedback Processes

To have an impact on an organisation, the Enterprise Data Models cannot be buried somewhere in a Knowledgebase or 'Architects-only' tools that are isolated from its operations and delivery processes. The definitions that are contained within the models need to be *all pervasive*, and this is never more critical than for any IT related activities.

Obviously to be influential, the models' definitions need to feed into any change processes within the system landscape, through effective mechanisms[19].

19   These mechanisms are examined in more detail in the 'Organisational Agility' chapter.

However, a key part of corresponding processes, should also be to include any feedback of *appropriate* changes, from the more specific models, to the more abstracted levels. These scenarios can arise, for example, where more detailed understanding in particular areas may be uncovered, or new data sources are consumed by the organisation.

***Principle 69***     ***Only modifications that have a <u>more generalised significance</u>, should be incorporated into the more abstracted models from more specific models.***

Principle 69 states that changes to the more abstract level should only be made, where the variation occurs, or could be reasonably expected to occur, in a significant number of repetitions of models at the more specific level.

As an example, consider a new 'Agreement Proposed Start Date' Attribute that is defined due to a specific implementation. If this Attribute is assessed to have an *Enterprise* wide significance[20], then it would need to be added to the highest level Enterprise Logical Data Model. Notice the key role that abstraction plays in determining whether our Attribute has more universal applicability.

Note also that these feedback loops indicate that the models themselves will *never be finished or static*, but must have a *limited* degree of *evolution* going forward.

***Principle 70***     ***As with all parts of the Idealised Models of an organisation's operations, the Enterprise Data Models must evolve over time.***

As a consequence of principle 70, the feed-forward and any corresponding feedback mechanisms, need to be factored into any managing process definitions. We will return to this requirement later in the book.

---

20    This is an example where the consensus from Business and Operational Stakeholders is critical in making informed judgements.

## Stakeholder's Relationships with Enterprise Data Models

What has been conspicuously absent from the discussion so far, is the way that the organisation's stakeholders interact with the Enterprise Data Models. The Enterprise Data Models *must* represent the collective understanding and agreed *meaning* of the data by the stakeholders of an organisation. This forms the basis of principle 71.

---

***Principle 71***    ***The effective involvement of key stakeholders and SMEs is absolutely critical to successfully define and maintain the abstract Enterprise Data Models.***

---

Wherever key stakeholders and SMEs are able to convey an accurate understanding of this understanding, they must provide detailed input, and be part of any review processes of the models. This is illustrated by figure 31.

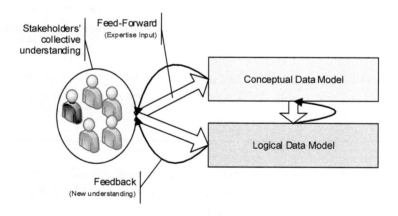

**Figure 31 – Stakeholders' relationships with the abstract data models**

This doesn't mean that they will be seen poring over detailed data model micro-structures. But nonetheless, the activities described in principle 72 must take place, if the Enterprise Data Models are to be successful in transforming the data benefits for an organisation.

> **Principle 72** *If Data Models are to be of maximum benefit for an organisation, processes that provide crucial stakeholder input need to be created - and adopted!*

Notice also that in figure 31, feedback can take place from the models to the stakeholders. This can happen for many reasons, such as when the modelling process has uncovered new patterns, domains, or data structures, of which the stakeholders were previously unaware. Challenging the assumptions and constraints articulated by stakeholders, can also result in enhancing *their* understanding.

## Data Dictionaries

We must be sensitive to the fact that most of our stakeholders, will not have a working knowledge of the visual syntax used in our structural data models. But, we *must* unlock the meaning contained in these models and share it with them.

Data Dictionaries provide useful ways of communicating data structures to an audience that cannot read visual data models. To provide maximum benefit they need to be concise, accurate and contain useful descriptions to verify a shared understanding of the data.

> **Principle 73** *The descriptions, structures and definitions of the data elements in any Data Dictionaries need to be consistent with those held in the Logical Data Models.*

What principle 73 determines, is that the definitions need to be directly related to those contained in the Logical Data Models. This linkage provides assurance that the Enterprise's data meaning is delivered into the system landscape.

Often, Data Dictionaries are also seen as valuable for more development-focussed activities because, for example, they can be used to easily create new physical data structure definition scripts. As a result, they tend to be system implementation-centric, and therefore tend to contain more *localised* definitions than their related Enterprise model counterparts.

As long as they have, for example, table names, column names and data types recorded, many of their consumers are satisfied. However, as we shall see in the next section, they should be considered in the wider context, and so need to be more fully defined to yield maximum benefit.

## Enterprise Data Lexicon

Whilst not a model per se, a key component in the suite of Enterprise Data Models is the Data Lexicon. The Data Lexicon provides reference definitions that are entirely consistent with the visual structural data models, but provides an alternative and complementary communication mechanism.

Data Lexicons are defined most successfully at the Enterprise level, and therefore their definitions must be agreed across the organisation[21]. Importantly, they must contain definitions that are abstracted from any implementation specifics and reflect the operational or business understanding of the data.

The use of a Data Lexicon can often be more appropriate than using structural data models for review by stakeholders.

> *Principle 74*    *The Enterprise Data Lexicon must be formed from the agreed definitions of data, and provides a reference that can be used to facilitate common understanding across an organisation.*

The relationship between the Data Lexicon and Data Dictionaries is illustrated in figure 32.

---

21    With the caveat that they may use synonymous terms more familiar to certain areas of the organisation.

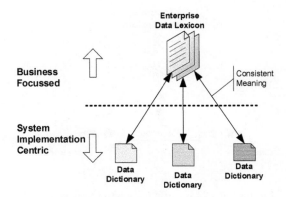

**Figure 32 – The Enterprise Data Lexicon and Data Dictionaries**

Typically, Data Lexicons are not single documents, but instead comprise a collection of some, or all of the related artefacts:

- Enterprise Data Dictionary/ies

- Enterprise Semantic definitions

    o a catalogue of meanings, examples and abbreviations

    o synonyms and regional or colloquial terms

    o Taxonomies of terms

- Data Lifecycle definitions

## Conforming Understanding

By disseminating the understanding of the Enterprise Data Lexicon's definitions, we can begin the process of conforming understanding. This conformance, is the primary benefit that the Enterprise Data Models deliver. It makes their definition and dissemination an essential pre-requisite for deriving the maximum benefit from an organisation's data.

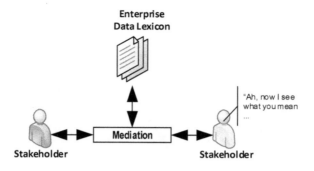

**Figure 33 – "Ah, now I see what you mean …"**

Figure 33 provides a simple schematic representation, of the rationale for the creation of a Lexicon, as indicated by principle 75.

> *Principle 75* **An Enterprise Data Lexicon is essential as a reference tool for all stakeholders, since it forms an independent point of reference that conforms the data definitions used in stakeholder's communications.**

This process of conforming stakeholders' understanding, will reduce the barriers to understanding across the organisation, and can enable *all* stakeholders to have a common foundation for their collective decision making.

> *Principle 76* **Establishing a conformed <u>conceptual</u> landscape, using an organisation's Enterprise Data Models, starts to create conformance in the way that stakeholders think, the concepts they understand, and the terms they use.**

The question that we need to answer by the end of this book is; how can we possibly disseminate the Enterprise Data Models into the realm of development, in a way that will enable us to gain the maximum benefits from them?

# 4: The Seven Principles Of Data

*Our organisations require a simple guidance framework to validate their data related decisions in this era of exploding innovation.*

Today, the white heat of Big Data's impact is beginning to cool and its associated expectations and technologies are beginning to mature. And yet, we are being assailed by new waves of seismic change; Artificial Intelligence, Blockchain and Machine Learning, to mention a few.

Strangely though, even though we are in an era with more abundant data than ever before, in any new realms, our data related decisions may become increasingly arbitrary!

This is because the time available to understand the impact of each innovation constantly decreases, whilst their complexity constantly increases.

How can we expect to make rapid decisions that are strategically sure-footed, when we have diminishing experience on which to base them?

What we need in the uncharted territories we are entering, is a very simple set of overarching principles to provide a firm foundation for our decisions - a data compass if you like.

This chapter defines seven such principles that we can apply to all data related changes. If we ensure that our data related decisions achieve positive outcomes from these principles, then we have a way of maximising the ongoing success of our organisations.

## What Are The Seven Principles Of Data?

This book contains many principles, concepts and models, to ensure long term data benefit for organisations. These act as guides for our day to day data related decisions.

But what about the more strategic and over-arching decisions. We cannot assess these by referencing the many low-level building block principles of Data Architecture. Instead, we need a handful of simple, high-level principles that we can use to reach our decisions. This chapter describes seven high-level principles that we should use.

The Seven Principles of Data are:

0. Achieve Sustainability

1. Increase Convergence

2. Increase Conformance

3. Increase Coherence

4. Improve Agility

5. Reduce Risk

6. Improve Data Flows

7. Improve Data Quality

These are described in more detail in the following sections.

## Principle 0 - Achieve Sustainability

The Achieve Sustainability Principle, is cheekily actually the Zeroth Principle. The Achieve Sustainability Principle underpins all of the others and therefore is the *root* Principle of the other seven.

---

*Principle 77*  **Sustainability is achieved, by achieving the overall net positive outcomes from the Seven Principles of Data and is thus the root principle.**

---

This principle states that, whatever is chosen as a course of action, needs to be based upon the benefit to an organisation being outweighed by the cost[22]. Importantly, this judgement has a long term perspective. So even if the cost outweighs the gain initially, it is the longer term *net* gain that is key.

---

22   Cost here refers to resource expenditure rather than purely financial.

> **Principle 78**   **All decisions need to be made on the basis that they improve the ongoing _sustainability_ of an organisation.**

It can also be seen as a re-interpretation of the organisational fitness model developed in chapter 1. It ensures that all effort is directed to activities that yield maximum long term net benefit for an organisation. It should also determine that effort wasted on worthless activities becomes eliminated.

## Principle 1 - Increase Convergence

The Increase Convergence Principle dictates that decisions need to be taken with the objective of improving convergence towards the Idealised Models. This Convergence refers to the _infrastructure_ of the Data Landscape. What we mean by infrastructure is the framework of the data's definitions and models and their associated real world processes and data related system landscape components.

> **Principle 79**   **All decisions need to be made to improve the _convergence_ of data, processes, their models and their systematised implementations.**

The Convergence Principle seeks to improve the alignment of the four quadrants of figure 17 on page 41.

But it must also be overlaid by the strategy of the organisation, as this pre-dominantly relies on data to bring it to fruition. The data and related activities must mesh harmoniously in both their representations in models, and their Real World counterparts.

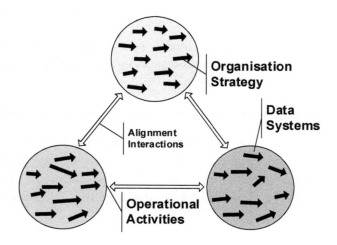

**Figure 34 – The Increase Convergence Principle**

Key parts of this alignment must be brought to bear on the organisation's data's *meaning* and patterns. As we have already seen in the preceding chapter, the definitions of the Idealised Models are, in large degree, specified within the Enterprise Data Models.

By increasing the amount of alignment with these, the convergence of system implementations will also be increased.

But how will we achieve this principle?

Design patterns at an Enterprise level can be used to converge technical solutions. The convergence achieved through system implementations, will cause a dramatic lowering of development and support costs. Therefore employing this principle will drive corresponding benefits for an organisation's system delivery capability, *and* its day to day operations.

## Principle 2 - Increase Conformance

The Increase Conformance Principle dictates that decisions need to be taken with the objective of improving the alignment of organisation's data *meaning* with the Enterprise Data Domains.

Whereas Convergence refers to the *infrastructure* of the Data Landscape, Conformance is concerned with the *meaning* of the data that flows through this landscape.

> ***Principle 80***     ***All decisions need to be made to improve the <u>conformance</u> of data with the Enterprise Data Domains.***

Put simply, Conformance will ensure that the data consumed from different sources across the organisation, will have consistent *meaning and language*.

It will also guarantee that data is fit for purpose within the organisation's processes, and .will enable improved and simplified systematised data exchanges.

By conforming an organisation's data definitions to its Enterprise Data Models, the organisation's systems will begin to have aligned patterns of:

- data definition and structures

- interface definitions

- data transfer semantics

For example, ensuring that the organisation's Product definition domains are agreed and shared across the organisation, will facilitate sharing of data and reporting consistency. In its absence, we have the situation where, although systems *can be connected* to each other, they are still unable to exchange data easily. This is because they do not share a common 'language' to represent the *meaning* of the data.

## Principle 3 - Increase Coherence

The Increase Coherence Principle ensures that the independent parts are consistent and integrated with the wider Enterprise-wide view.

> ***Principle 81***     ***All decisions need to be made to improve the <u>coherence</u> of data and processes across an organisation.***

If the entire scope of an organisation's data is defined within the Enterprise Data Models, then it is possible to deliver any individual parts of these definitions, within different systems, and at different times, *without* detrimental impact on the organisation's system landscape.

> **Principle 82**  *The Enterprise Data Models provide a 'big picture' of the data, which can be used to ensure <u>coherence</u> across separate implementations.*

For example, it is possible to easily combine data sourced from different systems, even if they were implemented at different times but based on separate, yet coherent, parts of the Enterprise Data Models.

Alternatively, new data structures can be added to extend a previously implemented model. As a result of each individual implementation being based on an area of the Enterprise Data Model, any subsequently implemented structures, will be coherent with the existing structures.

In other words, ultimately, the discrete components are guaranteed to snap together seamlessly like pieces of a jigsaw.

Immediately, we can see the benefit for our delivery teams. This is because different teams can work 'independently' on separate areas, secure in the knowledge that the separate delivered components will form part of a larger coherent system landscape. This coherence must be an essential pre-requisite for a Micro-services approach to delivery.

But we should not forget that this principle equally applies to the business and operational activities, and that these in turn must be part of a coherent set of pattern definitions.

## Principle 4 - Improve Agility

Agility is often thought of within the context of Agile development approaches. In fact, although these may help to a degree, the real step changes in agility derive from implementing architectural patterns.

The Improve Agility Principle ensures that these factors are taken into account in *all* relevant decision processes, especially those to do with the re-engineering of an organisation's underpinning systems.

> **Principle 83**    ***All data related decisions need to be made to improve the overall <u>agility</u> of the organisation.***

Another factor to consider is that due to the convergence of systems, the proportion of organisational budget allocated to support and maintenance, will be reduced. Lowering spend on these non-beneficial[23] maintenance activities, allows the potential redirection of resources, to adopting system innovation. This increase in an organisation's ability to adapt to change[24], also represents enhanced agility.

As we will see later, organisations will be able to implement and modify systems much more rapidly by basing them on patterns derived from the Enterprise Data Models. Hence, the models can be used to directly improve the overall organisational agility.

> **Principle 84**    ***Using Architectural patterns that are based upon Enterprise Data Models can significantly lower costs and development timescales, leading to <u>step changes in agility</u>.***

Listed below are a few examples of outcomes from applying principle 84.

## Fewer Moving Parts

More moving parts reduce an organisation's ability to make changes quickly. We typically think of moving parts as referring to components in system implementations. However, the concept of fewer moving parts is one that

---

23   Non-beneficial in the sense that the resources are expended to *remove problems* rather than actually *enhancing* the organisation's data capabilities.
24   This would be a good example of the concept described in chapter 1 that considered that fit organisations waste little effort on activities that yield no net benefit to them.

applies to almost all endeavours carried out by organisations.

Simplicity should be seen as a paramount objective to all Transformation and Business as Usual processes. There are many immediate benefits including ease of understanding and transparency. But we should consider that the overall *inertia* caused by complex and opaque solutions, can also be significantly reduced.

## Low Latency Processes

Organisational agility is all about being able to respond to change rapidly and with less cost.

> *Principle 85*   **It is essential to automate decision-making processes wherever possible, to reduce the waste caused by process latency and wait time across the organisation.**

This means that all processes, and in particular any data related decision-making processes, need to have rapid resolution[25]. To facilitate low latency, they should be implemented using simple, *unified* workflows. By reducing latency they accelerate processes.

As an important by-product, they also provide all stakeholders with the visibility and direct engagement that encourages communication and shared ownership.

We will revisit this principle later in the 'Organisational Agility' chapter.

# Principle 5 - Reduce Risk

All decisions need to evaluate the constraints that affect the risk profile of proposed data related changes, and attempt to reduce, or mitigate such risks.

---

25   Delays in decisions, guidance or feedback result in development costs and risks being increased.

> ***Principle 86***     ***All decisions need to be made to reduce <u>operational</u> and <u>delivery risks</u> for implemented solutions.***

Risks can be created in a number of different ways. Typically the following spring to mind: cyber-security, financial, operational or reputational risk. But there are many others. For example, adopting a new ETL technology for which there are few resources available, either internally, or in the external market place, can expose an organisation to significant risk.

Or again, moving on-premise systems to the Cloud, can introduce risk in many ways. Normally the driving factor for this trend is the cost reduction or availability of hosting organisation's capabilities and tooling. But this benefit comes with other costs. Careful consideration of ways to reduce the associated risks should be undertaken, with particular attention being paid to how to exit such arrangements.

However, by repeatedly implementing the same defined patterns, the way that they are implemented can become far more efficient and effective. We should not overlook that the repeated implementations will allow us to hone and improve their patterns.

As a result of these continuous cycles of improvement, the risks associated with implementing them again in the future, become further reduced.

Additionally, due to repeated delivery of patterns, the timescales and effort required for each delivery can be more accurately quantified. This leads to more realistic estimates for subsequent deliveries, which has a positive benefit in reducing their implementation risk.

The preceding points form the basis of principle 87.

> ***Principle 87***    ***Using established and successful patterns to form the basis of new delivery definitions, <u>removes the risk</u> that would otherwise arise from using novel patterns and definitions.***

As a consequence of this principle, the organisation needs to *mandate* the use of proven architectural patterns. This can have a profound reduction on delivery risk.

To maximise their benefit from a data perspective, these patterns need to be aligned with the Enterprise Data Models, which is the approach promoted by this book.

# Principle 6 - Improve Data Flows

The Improve Data Flows Principle assumes that if data is the lifeblood of the organisation, then any improvement of (appropriate) data flows, will deliver a benefit to the organisation's operations and its strategic decisions.

> ***Principle 88***    ***All decisions need to be made to <u>improve appropriate data flows</u> throughout the organisation.***

In a sense we can see this as a re-interpretation of the '*Known*' and '*Shareable*' principle we saw in the first chapter. To bring it to life, a couple of examples of this principle are called out here.

## Systematised Data Flows

Data flows are used to co-ordinate many parts of organisation's operations including, for example: Client on-boarding, ordering of Products, Payments and Product fulfilment. These activities can only be made effective by their underpinning data flows. Thus, this principle must be applied to the provision of systematised data flows to support all such activities.

## Producer-Consumer Agreements

We cannot allow flows to be un-controlled. A way to ensure appropriateness is to introduce the concept of Producer-Consumer Agreements. These specify that the producer must undertake a comprehensive detailed description of data that it provides to potential consumers. This would involve Data Profiles, Data Hosting, access controls and Data Privacy for example. These form the basic Terms and Conditions that are inherent in consumption of the data. Consumers must then agree to this contract, and abide by their undertakings. In addition they must provide feedback to the producer of any breaches from their side of the contract.

We will pick up this theme again and see how to make it real in the subsequent chapters.

But we must also make mention of the need to deliver appropriate data to drive informed and reliable strategic decision-making.

These data flows are more critical than ever, and continue to grow in importance when we consider, for example, the impact of: Artificial Intelligence, Machine Learning and the Internet of Things

## The Enterprise Data Models and Feedback Data Flows

Earlier we saw that the Enterprise Data Models must adapt over time to support an organisation in five years as well as they do today.

As an example, in figure 31 we see data flows that will allow the Conceptual Data Model to be adapted by feedback from detailed and ongoing work building and adapting the Logical Data Model. These are critical data flows and we will describe later exactly how we will construct and use them.

## Principle 7 - Improve Data Quality

Data Quality is of paramount importance. Simply put, the lower the data's quality, the less benefit it can deliver to an organisation. Any reduction in the quality of data reduces its usefulness, by blurring its meaning, and undermining any analysis based on it.

> ***Principle 89***    ***All decisions need to be made to improve the quality of the data that flows through the organisation.***

But precisely what we mean by Data Quality is not often considered.

We can *only* assess the quality of our data with reference to an agreed set of definitions of that data. These definitions in turn must be ones that support our organisation's operational and strategic needs. This set of definitions are of course the ones we need to define within the Enterprise Data Models.

Once the idealised definitions are agreed, we can then compare the data coursing through our organisation's arteries with them[26].

To make this a reality, simple techniques, such as recording the Data Quality Rules directly into the Enterprise Data Models should be used. These will act as a centralised set of definitions which, as an example, can be used to define Acceptance Criteria and Test profiles within the sphere of delivery.

There are many tools and techniques that are well established to monitor and report on Data Quality. A careful selection of one or more of these, is critical to the successful improvement of Data Quality. Naturally measuring Data Quality is essential, but it is what this monitoring triggers in terms of remediation processes that is key. We will look at effecting such processes repeatedly in the following chapters.

## Delivering The Principles

Because the Enterprise Data Models contain an agreed framework of definitions of our data, they must form the cornerstone enabling the Seven Principles of Data to prevail in our organisations.

The transformations that the Enterprise Data Models can deliver to our data and system landscapes, can be dramatic. They are able to achieve this,

---

26    Refer back to page 25 where we described an organisation's Idealised Models and feedback processes.

by delivering the basis for all of the preceding Data Principles.

> ***Principle 90***    ***The Enterprise Data Models must be used to underpin the changes required by the Seven Principles of Data and thus deliver enormous benefits from an organisation's data.***

This sounds great, but the question it raises is, how can we make this a practical reality?

## Architectural Design Patterns Driving Design

The Enterprise Data Models can be used as the basis of Enterprise-wide design patterns[27]. These design patterns can, in turn, be used to create re-usable components that can then be implemented across an organisation's system landscape. This approach provides an extremely powerful tool for the organisation, by: aligning, streamlining and delivering true system agility!

Figure 35 illustrates how the Enterprise Data Models can be used to derive design *patterns*.

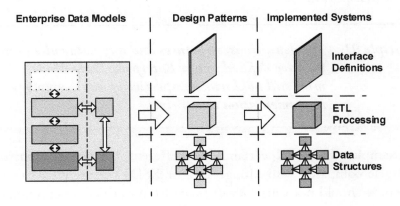

**Figure 35 – Enterprise Data Models driving architectural patterns**

Not only will this yield real benefits in terms of overall organisational agility, but it will also drive the consistent propagation of the data's shared *meaning* across an organisation's systems.

---

27   Note that these patterns will implicitly have a high degree of re-use.

Moreover, this approach will ensure that the data's *meaning* will be conformed in all technologies of the system landscape. But more than this, in addition to being agnostic from technology, this meaning conformance must be enforced for both Data at Rest and Data at Flow.

This requirement is illustrated conceptually in figure 36.

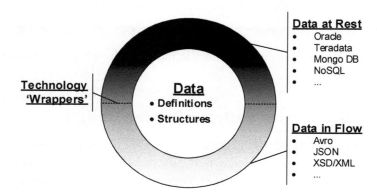

**Figure 36 –Technology-agnostic and 'Wrapper'-agnostic data *meaning***

What this schematic makes clear, is that the definitions and structures of our data must remain inviolate, no matter what technology is used to either store or transport them.

| | |
|---|---|
| ***Principle 91*** | ***The definitions, structures and any data rules that we have defined in our Enterprise Data Models must still hold true irrespective of any technology implementation constraints.*** |

For example, there will certainly be different technology constraints for Oracle compared with Mongo DB, or XSDs versus Avro. But these differences should not cause *any deviations* from our data's definitions and structures.

Only through this approach, can we retain the data's essence; the precious *meaning* that has been distilled and enshrined in the Enterprise Data Models!

Be careful here though! Many Technologists and implementation folk will assert that because we are using a non-Relational Database or self-describing data payloads, we can simply ignore the Logical Data Models. However, if our data is important to us, then we cannot allow this view to be influential. Obviously our Logical Data Models are more easily implemented in a Relational Database, but the models should have been defined from the business and/or operational understanding of our data. This understanding is key, and it must not be lost in an implementation. If it is, we face the high probability that the implementation's data cannot easily be shared across the organisation.

Also don't forget that even de-normalised implementations must equally respect our Logical Data Models.

## Deterministic Development Approach

The Deterministic approach to development, produces deliverables based upon the *declaration of what is required,* without the need to *define how to deliver it.*

| | |
|---|---|
| ***Principle 92*** | ***The Deterministic Development approach provides a way of radically reducing development effort.*** |

Instead of Software Engineers having to manually create the components to be delivered, they use Deterministic generation from meta-data repositories to automate delivery.

Because this approach dramatically reduces the input required by Software Engineers, not only does it reduce waste, but it also improves accuracy – the delivered components have a higher degree of 'fit' to the requirements. In addition to the immediate benefits it also allows us to change the implementation mechanisms easily. For example, a generator used to deliver DDL from meta-data can also be adapted to implement the same definitions in HTML or other documenting mark-up languages.

By using the Enterprise Data Models and the principles from the preceding sections, gives us a way to bring the Seven Principles of Data directly into the system landscape. Let's look at a concrete example of this.

Recently I came across an example of a Software Engineer painstakingly manually coding Data Quality (DQ) rules in Hive HQL, using an emailed text document as the 'source of truth' for the definitions!

I suggested that we create a simple generator instead. This was driven from a handful of meta-data tables which were populated with the DQ rules directly from the business definitions. The DQ HQL code used to implement the rules was literally generated in seconds. But importantly, because it was generated deterministically, the DQ checks were created *accurately.*

As the DQ Rules changed, the meta-data was simply updated and then the DQ checking SQL re-generated. Effectively the whole process became self-service for the Data Quality Analysts who defined the DQ rules and analysed the results.

Obviously, this provides us with the ability to respond quickly and accurately to change, and hence boosts agility. Additionally, using the meta-data tables, provided a *shared* visibility of the DQ rules.

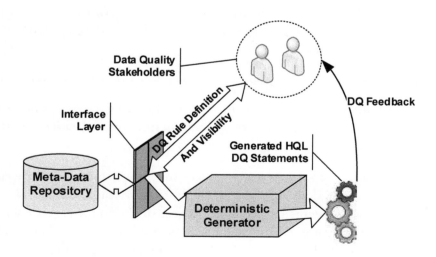

**Figure 37 – Deterministic infrastructure generation**

The Software Engineer was freed up to make more interesting and worthwhile contributions to the delivery work-stream, much to their relief.

# 5: Agile Data Assurance

*Today, the only constant, is the constantly accelerating rate of change!*

In this era of ever increasing data turbulence, what remains paramount is the need for our organisations to insulate their data's *meaning* from the constant stress they experience.

To ensure that their data's meaning is resilient to the changes that buffet them, organisations need to implement a well-defined, coherent and consistent framework of management processes.

Typically, such a framework is called a Data Governance Framework.

In parallel to the way that the definitions of its data must reflect the organisation, the Data Governance Framework must also be integrated with its prevailing culture, internal structures and processes.

Hence, it is not possible to document a *standard* Data Governance Framework for *any* organisation. But, in this chapter we will describe the standard building blocks that can be adapted to construct one that is appropriate for a specific organisation.

If one doesn't already exist in your organisation, these building blocks will empower you to create it. Or, if one does already exist, this chapter will help you to identify possible enhancements to it.

Later in the book we will discover how these components can be assembled and made effective by meshing them with the organisation. If this can be achieved, it will enable the organisation to survive and thrive, in spite of the constant turbulence of its operational environment.

## Defining a Data Governance Framework

In all but the smallest organisations, there is an almost total reliance on systematised data. However, in the absence of effectively governing its data, an organisation is destined to struggle to deliver even the most basic benefits from it.

For example, within such an environment, there is a strong likelihood that an organisation's data will be isolated within silos. Also it will typically be mired in constant manual data mapping exercises, or costly and interminable remediation programmes for regulatory or other purposes.

We need to provide a way to address the many problems that can give rise to these types of symptoms. But this needs to be more than setting up review bodies, or regular conference-call forums.

A Data Governance Framework is the coherent set of processes, roles and artefacts that together provide the effective management of an organisation's data. If this can be well defined and implemented, then it can deliver a significant boost to the benefit an organisation can derive from its data.

Unfortunately, there is no magic formula for the specification of such a framework. Each organisation must evolve its own definitions. This is because, if the data's meaning and usage must reflect the organisation, so must the framework that manages it. Thus the framework must align with the culture, people and processes of the organisation.

| | |
|---|---|
| *Principle 93* | *A Data Governance Framework definition needs to reflect the specific characteristics of its organisation.* |

Obviously for maximum effectiveness, a Data Governance Framework must be all pervasive within an organisation. But of course, in a world of systematised data, there is nowhere more important to have real control, than the activities that change its system landscape.

| | |
|---|---|
| *Principle 94* | *The Data Governance Framework can only be fully effective, if it has direct control over __all__ changes to the system landscape.* |

In the next sections, we will describe what the framework needs to contain and how it should be structured.

## The Seven Principles Of Data As Foundations

The Data Governance Framework needs to be founded on sound architectural principles. Of course, the ones we will use are the Seven Principles of Data that we defined in the preceding chapter.

Their definition and adoption, *must* be agreed as a pre-cursor to the Data Governance Framework development and implementation.

---

**Principle 95**    *The Data Governance Framework must be based upon sound Data Architectural Principles, as enshrined in the Seven Principles of Data.*

---

In the absence of this foundation, the framework can drift into arbitrary, remote or possibly, personality driven outcomes, and as a result, lose its effectiveness and stakeholder commitment.

## Data Governance and the Enterprise Data Models

Effective Data Governance relies on universal definitions that act as points of reference within an organisation's data landscape.

In spite of this, organisations often implement a Data Governance Framework and yet completely ignore this fundamental concept. Obviously, if they do this, they are destined to never achieve the full benefit that could be delivered.

Such organisations will be only too well aware that their people, processes and systems are unable to effectively communicate with each other, and as a result, deliver compromised outcomes. This degraded delivery will result in a system landscape that remains largely unknown and untamed. All their change processes will become more difficult than they need to be, and the benefits will rarely live up to the promised expectations.

Unfortunately, the cause of these frustrations will not be clear to them, and thus the remedy will be similarly elusive.

It is the Enterprise Data Models that provide the required set of shared data reference points for any Data Governance Framework. Because they are based upon the stakeholders' agreed understanding of the data's meaning, they provide the objectivity for the framework.

---

**Principle 96**    *The basis of the Data Governance Framework <u>must</u> be the consensus of the organisation's understanding and definitions of its data, as defined within its Enterprise Data Models.*

---

When specifying a Data Governance Framework, these should be seen as a mandatory part of the defining framework. As a consequence, their integration and corresponding management processes, should be seen as critical to the overall success of the framework.

## Data Governance Aligning the Organisation

In chapter 1, principle 6 stated that to maximise data's benefit, Data Architecture must align the production, modification and consumption of it throughout the organisation. We can now refine this principle to support the Data Governance Framework requirements as in principle 97.

---

**Principle 97**    *The higher the degree of alignment of an organisation's organisational strategy, operations and data systems, the more effective, efficient and <u>agile</u> the organisation can become.*

---

Figure 38 illustrates the alignment between the key areas of the data landscape. What this schematic indicates, is that both the Data Governance processes, and the processes that deliver change into the system landscape, are the key players that orchestrate this alignment.

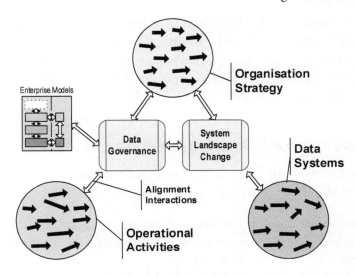

**Figure 38 - Aligning data across an organisation**

Notice though that this schematic also indicates a line of symmetry between the operational domains and the system delivery domains. It suggests that Data Governance naturally has an emphasis on the operational side. However, if it is to deliver its stated aims, it must also prevail over changes to the system landscape. We will see in the 'Organisational Agility' chapter, exactly how this influence can be guaranteed in a way that also boosts delivery outcomes.

Figure 38 clearly also indicates that the Data Governance Framework must interact with the overall organisational strategy. Importantly, it will need to ensure that the data landscape provides any required underpinning support of the strategy.

As the organisational strategy evolves, the Data Governance Framework must evolve in step, and thus remain relevant to the organisation's future.

| *Principle 98* | *The Data Governance processes must ensure that the data is managed in a way that is entirely consistent with the organisation's overall organisational strategy.* |
|---|---|

But there is another implication from this diagram, and it is that the Data Governance Framework should also influence the strategy. This can arise when its processes make discoveries as a result of driving change. For example, when investigating exit strategies for systems that the organisation wants to host using external Cloud providers[28].

# Data Governance Framework Goals

We've specified what the basis of the Data Governance Framework should be, but what should its goals be?

These must be based upon the Seven Principles of Data, but are framed by specifying concrete improvements. To illustrate such outcomes, we'll consider improvements to the following:

- Data Conformance

- Data Quality

- Organisational Agility

## Data Conformance

A way of measuring an organisation's systematised data conformance, is to estimate the proportion of systems that use conformed data structures and associated infrastructure. For example, did interface specifications make use of the Enterprise Data Model patterns?[29]

---

28    How we assimilate the changes that arise within the scope of development is described in the 'Organisational Agility' chapter.
29    We'll learn in the 'Organisational Agility' chapter how we can make the monitoring of such measures realistically achievable.

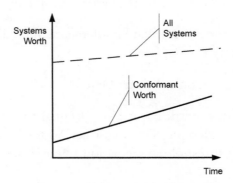

**Figure 39 – Increase in proportion of conformant systems**

Over time, the expectation is that the proportion of conformant systems' worth should increase, as illustrated in figure 39.

## Data Quality

A range of techniques needs to be employed, in order to assess the improvement in Data Quality. Typical ways of measuring Data Quality include:

- Reporting

- Profiling tools

- Data related defects

- Issues raised by data consumers

Careful Data Quality *specifications* need to be defined using categories such as:

- Uniqueness – removal of duplicates

- Conformance – correctly constrained to Domains

- Contemporaneous – interdependent values are accurate at specific points in time

- Completeness – all required elements are present at each stage in the lifecycle

- Compliance – evidence of regulatory compliance

It is also critical to define, record and implement simple Data Quality rules for the data, for example:

Contract End Date >= Contract Start Date

For many Data Quality metrics, it is also essential to set an *acceptable* data quality threshold. For example, 97% of Street Addresses must have a valid Postcode. Below this threshold, remediation activities need to be triggered.

However, don't forget that although simply measuring Data Quality allows you to establish how 'good' the Data Quality is, it is the implementation of processes that introduce corrections that is key! Rather than designing processes that need to make the same corrections over and over, it is better to design systems and processes that are able to adapt, and correct recognised errant data patterns. Better yet, if they can do this *without* human intervention.

Data Quality is typically of such importance, that many organisations develop a separate strategy and framework specifically for it.

| | |
|---|---|
| ***Principle 99*** | ***To maximise the benefit of Data Quality Strategy and Framework definitions, they must be aligned and integrated with the wider Data Governance Framework.*** |

# Organisational Agility

A core theme of this book is the improvement of the organisation's overall agility. An important part of improving this, is to reduce the construction and maintenance costs associated with all the data-related components of delivered systems[30].

---

30 Data related examples include; ETL Designs, Interface specifications and Physical Data Models.

**Principle 100** ***Organisational agility relies upon minimising the resources required to develop new capabilities for the organisation, and reducing maintenance costs for existing capabilities.***

Agility improvements will be boosted by the *re-use* of core patterns and components. This means that the agility benefits will not be dramatic during the period when the Data Governance processes are being established.

However, the gains will be increasingly apparent in the medium to longer term.

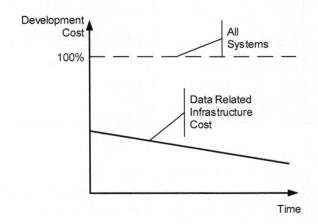

**Figure 40 – Proportion of data related infrastructure costs[31]**

We will be able to make the schematic view in figure 40 become a reality, by using the techniques covered in the 'Architectural Agility' chapter.

# Data Governance Maturity

One of the possible outcomes from you reading this book, will be to improve the maturity level of Data Governance in your organisation. But as with all successful journeys, defining the starting point is a pre-requisite.

---

31    Figure 40 represents the rebased estimation, of the proportion of Data Related Infrastructure costs, rather than an absolute monetary cost.

Therefore, being able to assess the current maturity level is key. We need this to be more than just a 'feeling', but in reality, formal methods for estimating it can be hard to make rigorous.

A possible thought framework for such assessment, is to consider the following three measurement domains and suggested coarse grain values[32]

| Domain | Description | Values |
|---|---|---|
| Data Governance Infrastructure | How prevalent are the *implemented* Process and Artefact definitions? | Non-existent<br>Low<br>Medium<br>High<br>Comprehensive and Rigorous |
| System Adoption | How prevalent are the Enterprise Data Governance definitions across the system landscape? | Adoption level<br>=<br>[Percentage within the system]<br>x<br>[The system's 'worth'[33]] |
| Adoption Determination | How determined is the organisation to make the Data Governance Framework universal and successful? | Zero<br>Low<br>Medium<br>High<br>Absolute |

If we imagine plotting the results of our assessments in a three dimensional chart as in figure 41, organisations that have a mature adoption rating would be somewhere at the back top right of this cube. Those in their Data Governance infancy, and indifferent to this fact, would be towards the front bottom left of the cube.

---

32   Consider making this a numeric evaluation, by assigning weighting factors to each of the measurement dimensions and coarse grain domain values.
33   This is a tricky one, but financial revenue or the potential costs of the risk the system mitigates (e.g. Compliance fines), could focus attention on the highest benefit areas for improvement.

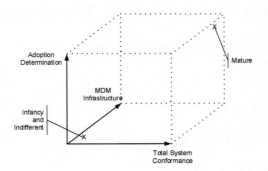

**Figure 41 – Data Governance Maturity Model**

This analysis can provide a useful way of characterising the current state of Data Governance and hence the starting point for any progression of your organisation's Data Governance Framework journey.

Let's now turn our attention to how the Data Governance Processes can be designed.

# Designing Data Governance Processes

The design of the Data Governance Processes, involves the specification of the universe of low level processes that together, comprise the overall Data Governance Framework.

Hopefully within your organisation, at least some of these will have already been defined! For these, all you will need to do, is integrate them with the delivery processes, as described in the 'Organisational Agility' chapter.

However, we can safely assume that there will be a requirement to create at least some of these, if not now, then certainly in the future. The following sections describe characteristics that need to be considered within such process designs.

## Process Design Template

To enable rapid, effective and consistent process definition creation, a standard specification template should be developed.

This template will include sections that mandate definitions of the following, for each process definition:

- All of the *relevant* Seven Principles of Data it supports

- Stakeholder roles and responsibilities

- Artefacts that act as

  o Input references

  o Output deliverables

- Workflow steps

- Decision points

- Success criteria

## Agents for Change

Agents for Change are those activities, or outcomes from activities, that need to trigger the Data Governance processes. Each of these will need to have a process workflow defined for it.

> **Principle 101**  **A key part of Data Governance process design, is to understand and document the Agents for Change, within the organisation's data landscape.**

Some of the high-level triggers for these are quite obvious, such as a new system delivery, or data migration to a new system. Others are more subtle, but still require some thought about how to respond to them. For example, an individual runs a query and discovers what they consider to be an anomaly. How will the Data Governance processes respond to this event?

This may be a scenario where the appropriate response is to invoke the 'Do we care?' test. This will assess how feasible, or desirable, it is to respond to these kinds of small events within an organisation. Would a simple Operational Support data defect tracking system be appropriate for such small Agents for Change?

## Determining the Agents for Change

Figure 42 illustrates typical primary Agents for Change. This schematic can be used as the basis for identifying the relevant Agents for Change within your organisation.

Each of these identified triggers needs to be considered as a driver for a process flow definition. However, after some analysis you may think that combining several as triggering the *same* process flow, makes good sense. Combining the processes will also simplify the workflows [34] and make them easier to assimilate.

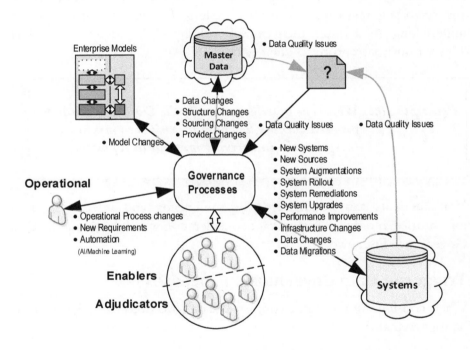

**Figure 42 – Data Governance process triggering events**

Figure 42 illustrates how triggering processes throughout the data and system landscapes, can in turn act as further Agents for Change.

When we consider how to integrate Data Governance with delivery activities, we'll revisit this model to ensure that the integration is made effective and *lightweight*.

---

34   See the 'Fewer Moving Parts' section on page 85.

## As Simple as Possible

Earlier, we saw that the Improve Agility Principle recommended the minimisation of moving parts.

This is especially applicable within the area of Data Governance where, for example, minimising the number of meta-data repositories will pay massive dividends. In the past, I have worked within organisations that have a bewildering array of disparate artefact repositories for their Data Governance Framework.

For these organisations, getting a holistic picture of their data landscape, and providing answers to even the simplest of requests, can be a major undertaking. As a result, their overall visibility of key definitions is lost. This seriously compromises their agility.

---

*Principle 102   Wherever possible, simplify the Data Governance processes, and a key part for this is to minimise or integrate the underlying meta-data repositories.*

---

Many benefits can be delivered by minimising and integrating these repositories, and this is a significant consideration when designing the Data Governance Framework.

## Triggered Data Governance Processes

When considering the framework's processes, we need to design them to be triggered at a:

1. Macro level - e.g. engagement with a new delivery work-stream

2. Micro level - e.g. amending an existing interface specification

New delivery work-streams such as Projects or Programmes, need to initiate their engagement with the Data Governance Framework. Once a work-stream has started to deliver, there will also need to be BAU processes in place that respond to the low-level changes triggered by the delivery. And inevitably, there will also need to be closure processes that wind down the work-stream.

The following schematic illustrates the way that these processes need to act as entry gatekeepers, BAU processes and exit gatekeepers.

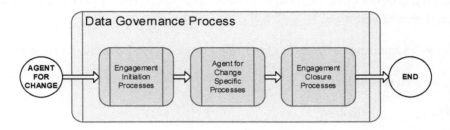

Figure **43** – Data Governance engagement processes

The entry and exit gatekeepers could be generic in design or be specific to the work-stream types such as; Agile, SDLC or migrating systems to the Cloud.

A few examples may help to bring this into focus:

- An Enterprise Data Model is extended due to a Business Acquisition

- New Accounting software is being adopted

- A migration of data from spreadsheets into a Client Relationship Management system is planned

In this book, we will need to consider in more detail, how system landscape changes will trigger such processes.

## Engagement Initiation Process

This process will define the way that the Agent for Change stakeholders engage with the Data Governance processes and exchange information including artefacts.

We will, of course, automate where possible, but for the Data Governance processes, there will still be a requirement to engage with people for at least some of the adjudication processes [35]. This means that a key part of the Engagement Process, must be to nominate individuals who will liaise between the various stakeholder groups.

---

35   At least for the next few years before Machine Learning and AI will make these obsolete!

At the macro level, it will be important to create the initial meshing of the two sets of processes. The Engagement Process would need to define and agree the overall process characteristics and outcomes. In particular, it will need to establish the:

- Outcome deliverables, including any Service Level Agreements

- Stakeholders'

    o Roles

    o Responsibilities

- Success Criteria

The process definitions should specify the overall style of the process mechanisms particularly to ensure that the processes remain on track and roadblocks are removed.

## Specific Agent for Change Process Definitions

At the micro level, the specific Agents for Change process definitions will demand the greatest part of the design effort.

Figure 44 illustrates a simple generalised process model that can be used to kick-start your definitions for each BAU process.

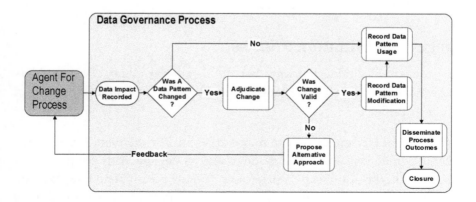

**Figure 44 – Specific Data Governance processes**

There is a lot more detail on how to complete the specific Data Governance process design, in the 'Organisational Agility' chapter.

Various metrics about the BAU processes should also be captured. These will provide important feedback data, monitoring the effectiveness and efficiency of the Data Governance Framework itself. They should be seen as key deliverables, and should include for example:

- Elapsed time – end to end resolution time

- Wait time – when the process is idle

- Total effort – combined hours for the stakeholder group

## Engagement Closure

As its name implies, this process brings the engagement to a close, and ensures that all the necessary tasks were completed, and documented. This is more relevant for SDLC Projects than Continuous Delivery work-streams at the macro level, but even Continuous Delivery work-streams will eventually be demised.

If any of the agreed engagement deliverables were not fulfilled, then the reasons why not, and any resulting impacts need to be recorded. These 'lessons learned' should then be made available to any similar work-streams in the future. This will contribute to the 'organisational learning' approach that this book champions.

Earlier, we considered that communication flows of the outcomes of all processes, need to be triggered. The closure process should also ensure that the outcomes from the engagement are correctly recorded in appropriate artefact repositories.

In order to facilitate this, the targets and dissemination mechanisms involved, need to be considered, for instance:

- Updating relevant knowledge-bases[36]

- Disseminating adjudications and changes[37]

---

36  Primarily the Enterprise Toolkit as described in the 'Organisational Agility' chapter.
37  These are described in the 'Organisational Agility' chapter.

Where outcomes from the Agent for Change processes, act as further Agents for Change, this closure process will need to trigger one, or more, other Agents for Change processes.

For example, the modification of a Domain of values, may trigger Data Quality processes to align the actual values in the relevant production systems, with the newly ratified Domain's values.

## Data Governance Framework Data Flows

In terms of data flows, what is less obvious, and often overlooked, is that the Data Governance Framework needs to *prevail in all the data related activities* of the organisation.

Therefore to be effective, communication flows from the Data Governance Framework processes, to *all relevant* stakeholders, is absolutely critical.

> **Principle 103** *Effective communication flows that disseminate the Data Governance Framework definitions, and any changes to them, is critical to its success.*

As an example, work-streams that have registered Data Privacy impact could be notified about any changes to Data Privacy legislation and the organisation's corresponding policy changes.

Monitoring feedback data flows is also critical, as they support the tuning of the Data Governance processes. These are the data flows required to support the continual improvement of Data Quality related activities and thus should be considered as essential.

## The Data Governance Framework Adaptive System

Looking at the feedback model in figure 11, in the first chapter, we saw that an Idealised Model is used to control feedback to a Real World system. We can re-use that conceptual pattern here, to understand how Data Governance provides an Idealised Model of how processes, and systems, *should* act on an organisation's data.

Note that this model assumes that the data flow processes can be modified in a way, to align them with the overall Data Governance principles and goals of an organisation. This could mean, for example, adding a Data Conformance capability within a Consolidation Data Hub to improve Data Quality[38].

Additionally, the Data Governance Framework definitions must also be able to respond to changing requirements and constraints over time.

The model illustrated in figure 45, is therefore more appropriate. This indicates that the Idealised Model must be able to adapt using an *appropriate feedback loop*.

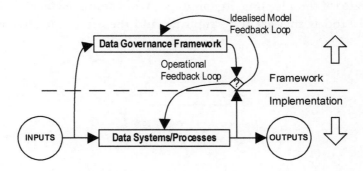

**Figure 45 – Feedback modifying Data Governance definitions**

As an example, imagine that an organisation starts to consume externally mastered data on its Clients, and integrate this into its Data Lake for reporting purposes. If this is a departure from its previous data use, it will need to extend the existing Data Governance processes to effectively manage this new data realm.

If we look at figure 45, the question it raises is; how we will assess whether the *modifications* to the Idealised Model are themselves *coherent* and *architecturally sound*. To resolve this conundrum we need an agreed set of architectural principles at a level of abstraction above the Data Governance Framework definitions. Of course, these architectural principles are the ones that we specified earlier and are enshrined as the Seven Principles of Data.

---

38    See the 'Managing Our Master Data chapter.

> **Principle 104  To guarantee the Data Governance Framework's long-term benefit to the organisation, any changes to it, must be based on the Seven Principles of Data.**

## Evolving Appropriate Data Governance Processes

When developing process definitions, we need to ensure that they are appropriate for the adopting organisation. Avoid defining Data Governance Idealised Models that are too simplistic, and therefore not effective as in figure 46.

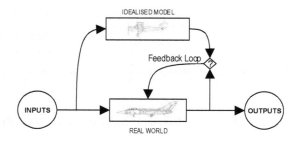

**Figure 46 – Idealised Model is too simple**

Equally, avoid developing Data Governance Idealised Models that are too complex, and therefore ignored by stakeholders as in figure 47.

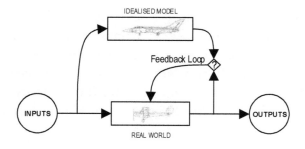

**Figure 47 – Idealised Model is too complex**

And what about the stakeholders?

## The Data Governance Framework Stakeholders

There are three groups of key stakeholders for a Data Governance Framework, and these are illustrated in the schematic in figure 48.

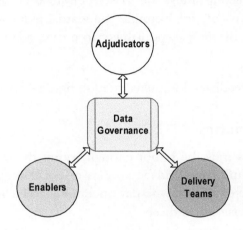

**Figure 48 – Data Governance stakeholders and processes**

The three high-level stakeholder groups are the:

- Adjudicators

- Enablers

- Delivery Teams

These stakeholder groups are described in the following sections.

## The Adjudicators

This tightly knit, core group of individuals, are authorized to make rules and key decisions regarding the definition and implementation of both the data under their jurisdiction, and also the framework itself.

### Aligning Data Governance and Organisation Strategies

It is critical for the Data Governance Adjudicators to also be closely aligned with those empowered to drive the organisation's strategies. The closer these are aligned, the more beneficial the Data Governance Framework can be to an organisation. A simple way that this can be achieved, is by ensuring that at least some of the Data Governance Adjudicators, are also in the group of Organisational Strategy stakeholders.

Their decision making must be based upon the Data Governance Framework in terms of, for example, standards, guidelines and policies. But, it is also part of their responsibility to create, adapt and *evolve* all of these as well.

This is where the feedback loop illustrated in figure 45 is crucial.

## Role Characteristics

These stakeholders must be senior enough within the organisation to be able to have real influence, and be able to effect change. However, they must be close enough to the day to day operations, to be 'in touch' with the impact of their decisions on these.

Importantly, they must also be committed, sufficiently incentivised and have adequate time available to devote to this role. Some upskilling of the stakeholders may be required to ensure that the adjudications and ratifications are based upon sound principles. Of course, the Seven Principles of Data should always be at the forefront of their minds!

## The Enablers

This team of stakeholders are tasked with carrying out the day to day operations that ensure that data is available, fit for purpose, and is aligned to the Data Governance definitions.

We tend to immediately think of the people required to keep the disks spinning and the network humming with data transfer, but we must not forget the conceptual and meaning definitions of the data. We need the corresponding specialists who can maintain and assure these definitions.

A significant part of the day to day operations, is the assessment of Data Quality and the discovery of data anomalies. A forensic approach to these, may rely on specialised Data Analysts and Data Quality teams. Additionally, there are many other operational aspects, such as; data retention, security, disaster recovery and archiving strategies, which are also part of this group's responsibilities.

## Role Characteristics

The role characteristics for the stakeholders in this group must primarily include those with SME knowledge of the data, to ensure that the meaning of the data is aligned with system implementations.

To provide operational support, stakeholders with a comprehensive range of technological skills will be required. These would typically include DBAs, network and ETL specialists. But notice that these skills are not within the delivery work-streams, but from a BAU process perspective. Even with the advent of DevOps, we cannot expect Pod Software Engineers to take on the many BAU activities that are required across an entire system landscape.

In addition, for the Enterprise Architectural input, Data, Solution, and Technical Architects will need some formal representation. In order to be able to analyse and ensure Data Quality and conformance, some of the stakeholders must also have strong forensic data analysis skills.

## The Delivery Teams

The delivery teams will have varied membership and role requirements dependant on the implementation taking place. Recently, we have seen the dramatic relative decline of custom development. Contemporary implementations are typified by '*Something* as a Service' and data migrations are more common than green-field development.

We need to carefully design our approach for the integration of the Data Governance processes with our delivery activities. Key aspects relate to the structure of the delivery processes and teams, and also the way that the development and delivery is parcelled up.

Because of the importance of these factors, and how we practically trigger the Data Governance processes, this topic is covered in much more detail in later chapters of the book.

# Federated Data Governance

For larger organisations, there may be a need to adopt a more federated approach, for example, where the Data Governance Adjudicators are regionally based. A centralised body with oversight and co-ordination responsibilities, will then act as a communication and adjudication hub for the overall function.

This yields the following important benefits:

- More regional sensitivity e.g. to:

    o Cultural variation

    o Local languages

    o Legal and regulatory frameworks

- Faster turnaround times for interactions with the localised bodies

- More people involved overall, and so improved quality of decisions

- Closer alignment to regional development, testing and support operations

The interrelationships between the Regional and central Data Governance Authorities is illustrated in figure 49.

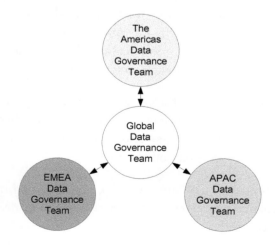

**Figure 49 – Federated Data Governance**

Notice that the federation depicted in figure 49 is along geographic lines, but it could equally be formalised along major organisational strata, such as Lines of Business, or Product Divisions.

## Enterprise versus Localised Definitions

As we saw earlier in the Enterprise Data Models chapter, there will always need to be support for a generalised scope, but that this generalised scope is more specific than the Enterprise level.

For example, their scope may be defined within a:

- Project/Programme e.g. Digital Marketing Programme

- Product e.g. Deposit/Loan/Insurance Products

- Regional jurisdictional e.g. EU Data Privacy

We always need to evaluate whether changes at a more localised level, actually represent patterns that need to be added at a more abstract, and, ultimately even at the Enterprise level. This is a key feedback process that enables the definitions to be effectively adapted to meet future re-use within the organisation. When designing our processes we must not forget this requirement and make sure it becomes built into them.

# Data Ownership

This is one of the trickiest aspects of Data Governance.

Many organisations attempt to simply allocate the Data Ownership to an individual role within the organisation, typically one that is represented within the Data Governance Adjudicators.

But can this work?

For example, who would own the data if it is mastered in ten different systems across the globe? Also, consider that making an individual accountable where they may have no power to ensure that changes become real in the system landscape, is prone to failure.

In reality, all three groups within the Framework have a *shared* responsibility.

And in fact, although we are concerned with Data Governance, other disciplines also need to be represented, for example: legal, regulatory and cyber-security.

If a single 'Owner role' needs to be created for organisational cultural reasons, then I suggest that the role will have the accountability for overall decision making. However, it must *achieve consensus* about the definition, maintenance and consumption of the data, with a wider group of defined stakeholders. This wider group must include influential representation from each of the relevant governance stakeholder groups.

Only a joint ownership model, can successfully take into account all of the different viewpoints of the data landscape, and also ensure that any desired changes become a part of the system landscape.

## Data Accessibility

Data accessibility refers to who gets to see, create, store, modify and delete data. This typically includes areas such as:

- Data Privacy

- Data Hosting

- Chinese Walls

  o Internal

  o External

- Authorities and Entitlements

This aspect of Data Governance is critical, and due to its importance, needs to well defined, and tightly enforced.

Some of the rules that the Data Governance Policies define will be to do with simple aspects such as Data Privacy, or data transfer between sovereign states. More complex Policies may be required for compliance with regulatory requirements, and these are typically subject to constant change.

Of special consideration, is how the data accessibility will be managed across the organisation's entire system landscape? For example, if key authorisations for a User are changed in one system, how will this change propagate across the other parts of the system landscape?

Some mechanism will obviously be required for this co-ordination, but this is not a simple problem to solve. It will typically involve a range of stakeholders, and potentially modifications to many systems.

However, the Data Governance Framework should only act to formulate the Policies, and ensure that adequate processes are in place to validate that the Policies are being implemented effectively.

The day to day detailed management of, for example, the Roles and Access Entitlements, would swamp the processes of the Data Governance Framework. Therefore, these need to be managed at a more granular, and localised level.

## Identifying Mastering Systems

As a pre-requisite to implementing a Data Governance Framework within an organisation, we *must* catalogue which systems are mastering which datasets.

This means that one of the first steps in the adoption of Data Governance, should be to define a simple matrix that cross-references the Conceptual Data Model high-level Entities with their Mastering Systems.

This will yield a great deal of easy to assimilate, high-level management information about the existing data and system landscapes.

> *Principle 105*   *A crucial preliminary step for organisations adopting a Data Governance Framework, is to catalogue the systems that create and manage their data.*

If an organisation's data and system landscapes are not documented as in principle 105, it is difficult to see how processes can be devised and implemented to take control of its data! Of course we will also need to accurately track any changes to the original catalogue to ensure that its data does not become stale and therefore of little value.

## Ratifying Golden Sources

Mastering Systems are known in many organisations as Golden Sources.

Careful thought needs to be given to how we certify Golden Sources. The stakeholders involved, must be close enough to the data and the processes that control it, to be able to agree on its authority as a Golden Source. In order to make this process have a degree of rigour, we should ensure that there are a standard set of criteria that are used to assist the judgement process. These might include, for example its 'guaranteed' Data Quality profiles.

A key part of the standard set of criteria, should be the responsibilities incumbent on any consumers of the data. For example consumers of Client data must undertake appropriate compliance with Data Privacy legislation.

At a minimum you may want to consider the following criteria domains.

| Area | Impact |
|---|---|
| Access | Who is allowed to see what elements of the data in the live system? Data Privacy is obvious, but don't forget to take other areas into account, such as, Commercial sensitivities and Chinese Walls. |
| Quality | A defined set of Data Quality undertakings for the data. |
| Retention | How long should the data be retained by consumers – the answer *might be* 'not at all'. |
| Privacy | What are the regulatory and legislative privacy constraints (across the globe) on how the data is used by consumers? |
| Hosting | Can the data be moved outside of its Country of jurisdiction? |
| Profile | What are the contents of the data being produced? For example is it EU data? Is it only the last two months' worth of online sales? Which Product/Services? |
| Periodicity | What are the periodicity constraints? For example, is it quasi-real time or monthly snapshots? |
| Development Usage Constraints | When development or testing takes place for the consumer system, must the data be synthesised, or masked in secure development and testing environments? |
| Modification Rules | Must the data's original values be preserved by consumers, or can they be augmented/modified? |

To reduce the burden of the Golden Source ratification process as a centralised function, we should also consider federating such adjudications. This will allow the processes to scale within larger organisations, and take into account local variations.

Changes to any of the above constraints over the data, need to be communicated with all the consuming systems, and this should be a responsibility of the Golden Source 'owner'. This needs to happen early enough for consumers to make any adjustments to cater for the changes, or register objections to them. It may be that a veto approach is adopted here, or where compliance is key, the changes are made irrespective of objections - and then help provided to mitigate the fall-out!

### Consumer Undertakings

Consumers of the data need to provide an undertaking to honour the constraints on the data usage as per the above elements. In addition, they must periodically review their usage of the data to ensure that they haven't contravened any of the original undertakings of its use.

The consumers need to also provide feedback especially around Data Quality breaches. Other areas for feedback include, for example, suggested changes, or enhancements to the data, including new Attribution.

## Data Lineage

Once Golden Sources are identified, high-level data flows from these to their downstream consumers, should be documented as a part of the definitions of the data and system landscapes.

The definitions of the data flows from source to destination, are often described as Data Lineage.

> **Principle 106**  **As a pre-requisite for effective Data Governance, it is critical to establish the Data Lineage flows throughout an organisation's system landscape.**

All new systems that consume data from upstream mastering systems and provide it to downstream consumers, should also take into account the need to support Data Lineage. Therefore, the documentation of any such flows, should be a standard requirement for all new system implementations.

It is worth investigating software options to track Data Lineage. There are an increasing number of products that are able to connect into databases, interpret their data catalogues *and* map the flow of their data from producers to consumers. Their adoption will remove the manually intensive and error-prone processes that are otherwise required, to maintain an accurate definition of the Data Lineage.

## Data Governance and Data Management

Just before we finish describing the Data Governance Framework, we should consider one important feature of it.

Data Governance and Data Management constitute a pair of complementary functions within the Data Governance Framework. As a result, they should be implemented with very close links and processes.

1. The Data Governance processes manage the rules, and adjudicate over anomalies and inconsistencies.

2. The Data Management processes provide custodial services for the data, and also implement the rules, and enforce the adjudications.

The following schematic illustrates the special relationship with which these functions need to operate.

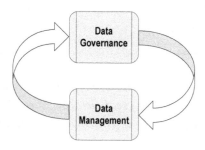

**Figure 50 – Data Governance and Data Management processes**

Even in the absence of any other Agents for Change, these two functions would still need to interact. This is because the Data Governance processes will need to continually evolve. For example, they will still need to respond to:

1. Organisational changes and external influences such as regulatory requirements

2. Data Management processes e.g. Data Quality

Some organisations have separate reporting lines for these separate aspects of Data Governance, but actually it makes a lot of sense to tightly integrate them.

# 6: Managing Our Master Data

*To maximise the benefit from our data, it is absolutely critical to implement effective management of its meaning framework.*

Almost all organisations these days have 'implemented' Master Data Management (MDM), and yet what they mean by this is often very different. For many of them, implementing MDM simply means having a central repository of their Clients and Products.

In this chapter, we'll look at a more holistic definition of MDM and see it is really a core part of the Data Governance Framework. It is the part dedicated to the management of an organisation's *context* data, and as such, it constitutes the *meaning* framework of the organisation's data.

Since, we have already considered the Data Governance Framework in some detail, many of the aspects of MDM, have already been covered. Therefore, this chapter describes the features of MDM that distinguish it from the overarching Data Governance Framework.

There is no silver bullet for implementing MDM, and the way that MDM is defined, will say as much about the organisation that embraces it, as it does about MDM as an abstract set of concepts and process definitions.

Nonetheless, for it to be effective, MDM processes must have a *real* control over the day to day operations that involve an organisation's Master Data.

Many MDM tools are readily available in the market and promoted as being able to *embody and implement* MDM for an organisation. Whilst this promise is undeniably seductive, there are a number of considerations that need to be taken into account when evaluating an MDM tool's true benefit. This chapter provides some possible challenges that can be used in the selection process for an MDM tool.

## What is Master Data Management?

Both Big Data adoption and Regulatory compliance have been drivers for organisations to recognise the importance of their Master Data.

The more enlightened organisations also realise the key role of Master Data in supporting and improving their day to day operations.

At the very start of our journey, we discovered that data requires a meaning framework for it to have a shared communicable significance. This allows it to provide benefit by giving it context. A major part of this meaning framework is its Master Data.

Without adequate control over this, the value we can derive from our data becomes rapidly diminished.

Of course, in order to enforce this control, requires the definition and execution of effective MDM *processes*.

> **Principle 107  Master Data Management is the defined framework of stakeholders, processes and artefacts that provides effective management of Master Data to increase its benefit to an organisation.**

Some organisations fail to grasp the important consequences of principle 107, and assume instead that simply implementing an MDM *tool*, will somehow *create a successful implementation* of MDM. To get a grasp of this, look at the Agents of Change in figure 42 and assess which of these would have an impact or dependency on Master Data. Then think how a tool would assist in bringing managed changes for the corresponding Master Data.

We must remember that tools can allow us to *execute* actions on our data, but in no way is this equivalent to delivering the total picture of what MDM should constitute. Simply implementing a tool *without* adequate *processes* wrapped around it, will certainly lead to a failure in delivering the concrete benefits of which MDM is capable.

> **Principle 108  To deliver real benefit, MDM needs to exercise an all-pervasive control over an organisation's interactions with its Master Data.**

There is another, and potentially more corrosive type of failure. This can often arise because the underlying enablers of principle 108 are overlooked. Many organisations think that as a result of simply creating artefacts and review bodies, that somehow they have implemented MDM.

But these are not the same as well thought through, integrated and *executed* processes!

This is a more subtle type of failure, since all stakeholders will assume that MDM *has* been implemented successfully. They will therefore not realise that they have not derived the full potential benefits that MDM can bring.

## What is Master Data?

In order to understand the scope of MDM, we need to look closely at exactly what we mean by Master Data.

In chapter 1 of this book, we learned that data measures and describes what is happening in the Real World. Also, we saw that it can only be of use, if an organisation can apply a context and meaning framework around it.

Master Data enshrines the vast majority of this meaning framework.

> *Principle 109  Master Data provides the core of an organisation's defined and agreed framework of meaning.*

Because it constitutes the meaning framework of an organisation, it can also be considered to contain much of the organisation's Intellectual Property. This re-emphasises the importance of, and the potential benefits from its effective management.

In simple terms, we can think of it as an organisation's:

- Reference Data and Master Data

- Meta-data

These can be considered the organisation's *domain* data. But is there actually a difference between these terms, and how do we determine what falls into the scope of MDM?

## Transactional versus Master Data Entities

The dividing line between the Transactional data and the Master Data in organisations is not an absolute.

As a result of creating data frameworks for many organisations that have different operational processes, it becomes clear that one organisation's Transactional data could be viewed as another organisation's Master Data.

This may seem a strange idea at first sight, so let's look at a simple example.

For some organisations, the creation of a Customer is almost always associated with each sale. This makes their view of a Customer quasi-transactional. For other organisations, their Client base is actually very stable and therefore their list of Clients can be treated as stable Master Data.

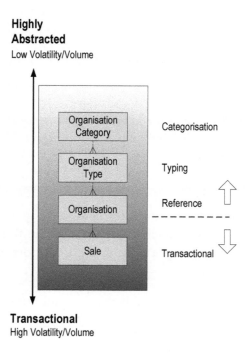

**Figure 51 –Transaction Data and Master Data spectrum**

This gives rise to the idea that actually there is a spectrum from the highest data volatility data to the lowest data volatility as illustrated in figure 52. It also raises the initially, somewhat counter-intuitive realisation that what we think of as Master Data, is simply the most slowly changing part of the Transactional data realm!

---

**Principle 110** *Master Data is the most slowly changing part of an organisation's Transactional Data.*

---

It is due to the permanent-ish nature of the Master Data definitions that they can be used to provide reference identities across the much more rapidly changing data that we typically think of as the Transactional data.

This means that where we draw the line for the delineation of Master Data on the spectrum is somewhat arbitrary. It will depend to a great extent on your organisation's operations.

## Master Data and the Enterprise Data Models

If Logical Data Models are rarely mentioned in discussions about the Data Governance Framework, I have *never* heard them referred to in terms of MDM. But, when you think about it, this is incredible!

How can the MDM Domains not be accurate reflections of the Logical Data Models' Domains[39]?

They must tell the same story about our data's definitions and structures. If we look at figure 53, this indicates an imperfect overlap between the Domains and Entities in MDM and those in the Logical Data Models.

---

39  Refer back to page 52 in the 'Data Modelling' chapter.

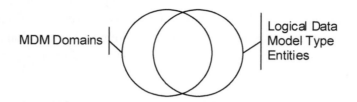

MDM Domains

Logical Data
Model Type
Entities

**Figure 52 –MDM Domains vs Logical Data Model Type Entities**

Immediately this raises a question we must resolve in our organisations. Ideally, there should be a total overlap between the two sets illustrated in figure 53. In most organisations though, this is not true.

This means that carrying out a very simple exercise to reconcile and align the two sets of definitions is amazingly beneficial.

> ***Principle 111*** *Every MDM Domain must be represented on the Logical Data Models, and every Logical Data Model typifying Entity, must be represented by a controlled MDM Domain.*

If this principle is not adopted in your organisation, then the resulting dislocation in the data's definitions will always cause wasted effort.

If setting up processes for the management of Master Data Domains, one of the first areas I would concentrate on is aligning the Enterprise Data Models with the MDM Domains.

## Master Data Management Data Scope

Notwithstanding principle 111, determining what falls under the control of MDM is harder than it sounds. Figure 53 illustrates that the scope of Master Data presents a complex, grey-scale landscape.

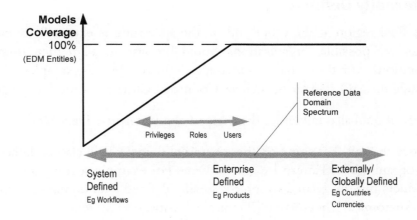

<figure>**Figure 53 – Reference Data spectrum**</figure>

This spectrum of Master Data, is also linked to the question of the subtle differences between Reference Data and Master Data. To do this, we will simplify the Master Data spectrum into three regions, as described below.

## System Defined

At one end of the spectrum, the domain data is highly system specific, and would include: user system privileges, reporting preferences, and workflow definitions, as well as any meta-data that controls these.

This includes Reference Data that is often characterised as being system Configuration Data. Typically, these domains would only be partly modelled in the Enterprise Data Models.

## Enterprise Defined

Some of the domain data has shared meaning across an organisation. This includes, for example, the range of Products and/or Services it provides. These need to be defined beyond individual systems, and thus they definitely fall under the scope of the Enterprise Data Models.

Nonetheless, their realm is bounded by the organisation scope. Internal Users and their organisational functional roles would fall into this category, since their significance is beyond individual systems.

## Externally Defined

The final region at the other end of the spectrum, is externally defined. Wherever possible, organisations would be wise to align their domain definitions, with those that are externally defined. Obvious examples of this include the ISO standards, such as: Countries, Currencies and Languages.

These should also fall under the aegis of the Enterprise Data Models.

Notice though that some of these external domains will also be linked to the organisation's Enterprise Master Data. For example, a company's drug Products may be related to internationally defined data domains, such as, the Anatomical Therapeutic Chemical Classification System.

## Inter-related Domains

Although we can typify the three regions, this analysis is a bit too simplistic. This is due to the fact that there are domains that provide links across them and thus, the picture of what should be Master Data, becomes far more blurred.

For example, Users of a system may correspond to People in the organisation domain. They may have organisational functional roles and system entitlements. These may control, for example: screen access, data access or specific workflow definitions. Quite obviously, some of these domain definitions are cross-system, but others are not.

Only domain data that is _not system specific_ should be classified as *Master Data*, and would typically fall under the MDM control.

> **Principle 112** **Only domain data and its associated meta-data, which has significance that is; cross-system or organisation operational, should be managed as Master Data.**

## Master Data Instance Management

Because of the importance of Master Data in enshrining the shared meaning of data for an organisation, it might seem self-evident to view each element as always having high intrinsic value, but is this true?

An important characteristic that determines the way that Master Data should be managed, is each *instance's relative worth* to the organisation. This relative worth has a spectrum as illustrated in figure 54.

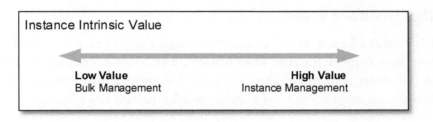

**Figure 54 – Master Data instance value spectrum**

In the interests of minimising wasteful processes, the management of each MDM Domain, needs to factor in the relative intrinsic worth of each instance.

> *Principle 113  MDM processes need to use appropriate management approaches for each domain of their Master Data.*

This important concept of the 'instance worth', is described in the following sections.

## Low Instance Value

If the worth to the organisation of each domain instance is low, then it only makes sense to manage it in simple ways across a multitude of occurrences. This may be relevant if the data refers to potentially millions of instances. For example, think of maintaining the details of each electronic ticket holder of a high volume transit system like the Seoul Metropolitan Subway. It makes little sense to devote significant effort to ensure that the details for *each* one are comprehensive *and kept current*.

Techniques that use bulk management of these domains need to be considered instead.

Often, where the Master Data relates to Peoples' details with a low instance value, getting them to manage their own details, is used as a cost-effective mechanism.

## High Instance Value

If the value of each instance is relatively high, then it becomes worthwhile to actively manage the data at an instance level. This is because the return on the effort is justified. This would be the approach to consider, if for example, an organisation has a stable set of relatively few Clients.

However, another factor to consider, is the impact of regulatory and legislative frameworks. These may determine that comprehensive and current data needs to be collected, *and verified*, about high volume Master Data that has low intrinsic worth. For instance, Financial Services regulatory frameworks, may require a degree of due diligence for new Clients, and further continual monitoring of existing Clients. Typically, this can exceed the level of effort that would be justified, purely on commercial grounds.

In the preceding cases, the relative worth of each instance is high enough, to justify continual maintenance of the potentially comprehensive data held about it.

## Dirty Domains

MDM Domains are the coherent sets of data that contain *defined* 'members', or data instances. For example, an organisation's Product Types.

Often when looking at the domain's actual values contained in the system landscape, we realise that they do not conform to the domain definition. They appear to have been lumped together, possibly because of system constraints, or lack of understanding, or care.

But, if we remember that it is only through shared and agreed meanings, that we can liberate the true potential of our data, this should actually be a hot topic![40]

---

40   Bear in mind though, that non-data folk may often be less able to enthuse about this!

Look at the following simple model in figure 55.

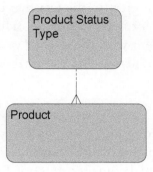

**Figure 55 – Simple Product Status Type Domain**

Imagine that as a part of our analysis we look at the Product Status Type values being supplied by mastering systems and we see the following data values:

| Product Status Type Domain |
| --- |
| Pre Launch |
| Development |
| Launched |
| Web App promoted |
| DEPRECATED |
| Old – DO NOT USE! |
| N/A |
| Other |

Oh dear!

We can see straight away that we have a problem in the data being provided that should have slotted nicely into our domain. It reveals two themes:

1. Muddying of the Domain values

2. Domain conflation

Let's take a look at what we mean by the above types of Dirty Domains.

## Muddying of the Domain

Muddying of the domain refers to the fact that insufficient care has been given to the analysis and/or implementation of the domain. Quite clearly the values reveal a problem with the *common understanding* of the domain, and therefore the appropriateness and sustainability of its values.

## Domain Conflation

The value 'Web App promoted' reveals a further symptom of lack of conformance to the definition of the domain. What it reveals is a *conflation* of values from two potential domains; those of Product Type and Product Status Type. This could have been prevented by a *clear*, *shared* and *agreed* *meaning* of the Product Status Type.

This is where defining the domains in the Logical Data Model can help to disambiguate the definitions.

# MDM Domain Management

Management of the MDM Domains is critical, because these form the vast majority of the *meaning* framework of the organisation's data.

This is a seemingly trivial aspect to Master Data Management, but in my experience, if well implemented, can yield enormous benefits. By contrast, if the processes of domain maintenance are flawed, it can result in difficulty to try to align data held in different systems. This can present significant barriers when trying to report across systems, or to aggregate the data into a centralised repository, such as a Data Warehouse, or a Data Lake.

> *Principle 114* **Processes that actively manage the MDM Domains, yield enormously disproportionate benefit compared to their cost, as these Domains enshrine the organisation's shared meaning.**

Inadequate controls can lead to costly remediation, through system update 'fixes' that constantly try to bring the data in production systems back into alignment.

But what about managing the values?

## Stakeholders and MDM Processes

The Agent for Change data flows in this relatively onerous set of processes, are illustrated in figure 56.

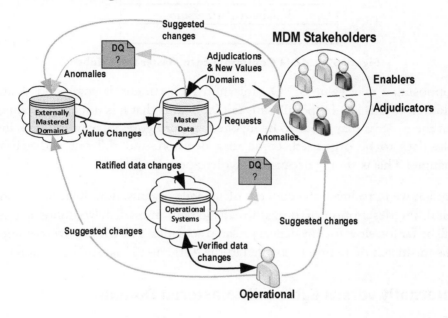

**Figure 56 – Managing Master Data Domain values**

The processes for these flows are difficult to automate, although we may see some progress in this in the next few years. At the moment, we still require humans to, review and interpret the data's meaning, and then conform it into a ratified set of values in each domain.

Something as simple as registering a new value for a domain, may take days to ratify. This is simply because of the time taken to:

1. organise meetings for the stakeholders

2. present them with the information they require

3. reach consensus

4. ripple any changes out into the system landscape

For example in the Organisation Formation Type domain, we may already have the values as per figure 57.

| Organisation Formation Type |
| --- |
| Public Listed Company |
| Private Company |
| Limited Liability Partnership |
| … |

**Figure 57 – MDM Conformance in Master Data Hubs**

Supposing a new value of 'Organisation Department' is suggested as an addition to this list. Hopefully, it is fairly obvious that it is not a valid value, but the process that needs to be invoked, as per figure 56, may still actually take days to be organised, come to a decision, and roll out and verify changes! This is simply because it involves people.

Earlier, we introduced the concept of an agile organisation. Bearing this in mind, the description of domain management immediately sounds like it will be far too slow for any delivery related activities. The trick to overcoming this mismatch of tempo is covered in the 'Organisational Agility' chapter.

## Internally versus Externally Mastered Domains

When we start to consider domains such as Organisation Type, we are immediately confronted by a realisation of something that is key within MDM. This is that MDM defines how the organisation views the environment in which it operates, as defined in principle 115.

***Principle 115  MDM enshrines the organisation's internal view of the internal and external Real World.***

Often people assert that Reference Data is simply Code-Description pairs, and that this is not the same as Master Data. However, this over-simplification ignores the point that beyond the ISO domains, such as Country, there is very little else that actually falls into this category. We only need to think about Industry Codes to recognise that even the selection of which externally defined domain should be used, relies upon decisions that are organisation-centric.

And even the much cited and simple Country Codes domain, will typically have links to the organisation's definitions of other geospatial data, such as Sales Regions. These extensions quite clearly provide an organisation-centric view of the Real World, and show how inextricably inter-twined the domains really are.

> **Principle 116**  *Although a great deal of MDM's meaning definition is a reflection of the Real World, it is the organisation's view of the Real World that is paramount.*

## Externally Managed Domains

In the same way that organisations are moving core system delivery to externally hosted infrastructure, they are similarly embarking upon out-sourcing of crucial Master Data Management to external organisations. In theory, the benefits are enormous. The reduction of people to manage the data, can yield significant savings to organisations.

In my experience, this approach is not always as beneficial as it initially seems. In many cases, the providers rely for their data quality feedback on the *consumers* spotting anomalies and mistakes in the data. There is also the need to ensure that the legal and Service Level Agreements are adequately specified to support the needs of the organisation.

This may not be quite as easy as it might appear, and can leave the organisation vulnerable to the provider wanting to change the: Terms and Conditions, or pricing structures, or simply ignoring key Data Quality issues.

And finally, the outsourcing creates a dependency on the external organisation, and this may not be as easy to reverse as it was to create. This is particularly the case, where the original savings in headcount resulted from the loss of expertise that can sometimes be impossible to replace.

## Master Data Hubs

Master Data Hubs (MDH) deserve special consideration within MDM due to the way that they are used in organisations. In this book, we will look at Consolidation MDHs. These consume data from multiple Mastering Systems, and then act as a single distribution point to multiple downstream consumers.

What the schematic in figure 58 illustrates, is that the MDM Processes should be used to apply Master Data conformance in the Mastering Systems' data. An important part of this is to align the MDM Domains wherever possible.

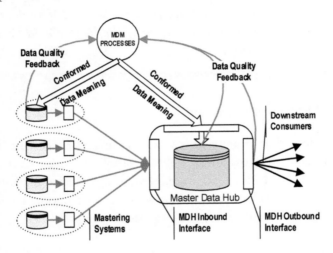

**Figure 58 – MDM conformance in Master Data Hubs**

In addition, if it has this capability, conformance needs to be applied through capabilities available within the MDH.

Notice that in figure 58 there are potential Data Quality feedback flows that may act as Agents for Change.

These can arise, for example, as a result of:

- continuous data quality checks
- verifying changes have been applied successfully

And, of course, these Data Quality flows need to have clear, prescribed processes defined for them.

### Data Domain Alignment

One of the key features of many MDM tools, is their ability to apply Data Quality regimes to the data that they master. Careful analysis should be undertaken as to how well they are able to support the requirement to propagate MDM changes directly to their consumers, as per figure 58.

## Master Data Management Tools

There are a plethora of tools 'badged' as MDM tools, and for many organisations the thought of a tool bringing their Master Data under control, is extremely attractive. However, as with all tool implementations, the tool in itself may not necessarily solve *any* problems.

---

**Principle 117   Master Data Management tools will not in themselves implement Master Data Management as a set of processes.**

---

Instead, we must focus on the *processes* that manage the data. The tool should only be thought of as providing *support* for these processes, and not as 'providing MDM' in itself.

## Considerations for MDM Tool Adoption

MDM tools offer increasing numbers of features that, for example, can apply advanced de-duplication algorithms to incoming data. This means that continually reviewing the available tools, *as a part of the* MDM processes, is a worthwhile activity in its own right.

But, we must remember that the adoption of a tool that is *poorly* aligned with an organisation's needs, may actually create a *hindrance* to the implementation of a successful MDM!

If we think of the MDM tool in this way, we now understand that it *may* be appropriate to adopt one, but there remain many questions to ask of how it could be integrated with the organisation's MDM Strategy and Processes.

Here are ten exemplar questions that could be asked in any MDM Tool evaluation:

1.  Can the success criteria for the adoption of this tool, be articulated and agreed at an organisational level?

2.  What are the *real* benefits of the MDM tool for *this* organisation[41]?

3.  What is the current level of the organisation's MDM maturity and is this consistent with the MDM tool's requirements and capabilities?

4.  How would the organisation integrate the tool with any existing MDM Strategy and Processes?

5.  Who would the consumers of its data be across the organisation, and what would be their access mechanisms to the information held in the tool[42]?

6.  How well will the tool integrate with other artefacts, knowledge-bases, systems and/or other tools e.g. Enterprise Architecture tools, Enterprise Models?

7.  How will the tool integrate with any existing organisational frameworks e.g. TOGAF?

8.  How will the tool be able to assist with managing consumption of externally mastered data?

9.  How will MDM meta-data be entered into the tool, and how will it be kept current, especially if process definitions change, for example?

10. How will the organisation's MDM processes be affected if the tool is upgraded or deprecated?

---

41   This is not, of course, necessarily the same as the tool's feature list! In other words, which specific problems does it solve?

42   Of particular importance, is how definitions and changes are disseminated across the organisation to all the levels of data related practitioners?

# 7: Architectural Agility

*Data Architecture must assure good data governance, but it must also deliver a dramatic boost to organisational agility.*

Before we step into this chapter and discover how to make our organisations truly agile, I'd like to share my favourite joke about Enterprise Architecture.

*"Thank you for calling Enterprise Architecture. Your call may be monitored or recorded for quality assurance purposes. Please listen to the following menu closely, as some of our options may well have changed.*

*• Press 1 for a 240 page document no one will ever read*

*• Press 2 if you have submitted a solution proposal for review weeks ago and had no response*

*• Press 3 if you would like a diagram which is unfeasibly complex and opaque*

*• Press 4 for a PowerPoint presentation which makes it all look 'oh so easy'*

*• Press 5 for an arbitrary decision which will drastically impact the delivery timelines of your project*

*• Press 6 to schedule a meeting where you can explain the problem again, to a slightly different group of people*

*• Press 7 to hear about how we solved it way back when we were responsible for delivery*

*• Press 8 if the central funding for a critical component of your application has just gone up in smoke*

*• Press 9 if you haven't got a Technical Lead, and need someone to micro manage project design issues*

*If none of these options cover your scenario, please send us an email and we'll respond during our next holiday, when we've got a free moment between conference calls."* [43]

Whether you think this is a funny joke or not, for many organisations there

---

43    I am not sure where this originated from, so apologies for not attributing it.

is a grain of truth in it. Their Enterprise Architecture function has become totally divorced from the other functions of the organisation, including those of system delivery.

The purpose of this chapter, is to suggest that Enterprise Data Architecture must not retreat into increasingly rarefied orbits. Instead, it must act centre-stage to co-ordinate and align all areas of the organisation.

If this can be achieved, it will bring all of the critical stakeholders back into effective communication as a positive by-product. This will deliver immediate benefits to each one, and hence to the organisation as a whole.

But how can this be achieved?

For many organisations, Data Governance is seen as a critical part of their operations. This is because, it acts to ensure compliance with legal and regulatory regimes. Arguably, we can view Data Governance as simply providing an *implementation mechanism* for Enterprise Data Architecture. As a result of this symbiotic relationship, we can deliver effective Enterprise Data Architecture, by using Data Governance as its Trojan Horse.

In addition, although the patterns we describe are framed within the terms of Enterprise Data Architecture, the same patterns can be re-purposed to provide other parts of Enterprise Architecture. Thus, they can also deliver a parallel direct impact on the organisation.

Before you can make this approach successful though, you may need to overcome a potential hurdle.

Often, Data Governance is seen as creating obstacles that only *impede* the delivery of the system landscape, and certainly it is not typically seen as providing any practical assistance. Actually though, this is not an intrinsic problem of good Data Governance, it is purely a symptom of poorly implemented Data Governance.

In this chapter, we shall see that this hurdle can be swept aside, because Data Governance can be used *to provide a step change improvement* in delivery, *and* still promote the wider organisational goals.

> ***Principle 118*** ***If Enterprise Data Architecture can be effectively meshed with delivery processes, it can provide a radical improvement in the delivery agility of an organisation.***

This chapter describes how we can dramatically improve both *delivery* and an organisation's *agility*.

## Architecture Driving Agility

In the early 21st Century, *agility* needs to be the Holy Grail for all organisations. Unfortunately for many, this is extremely difficult due to them being constrained by their systems.

In an attempt to free themselves from these system constraints, there is often a call to develop more stuff, more quickly and, crucially, using less resource.

Attempts to make system delivery more agile, have driven a recent radical shift to adopt the Agile and DevOps methodologies. And, to an extent, this response is a rational choice. This is because, as we all know, development effort introduces cost, delays and risk that can make delivery agility a pipe-dream.

But what is almost totally ignored, is the possibility that the required effort can itself be *radically* reduced by using architectural approaches.

Let's examine how this vision can be made a reality.

## Loosely Coupled Paradigm

To my mind, at the forefront of the architectural approaches, and *the* fundamental pre-requisite for delivery agility, is the use of a Loosely Coupled approach in the system landscape.

> **Principle 119** *An absolute pre-requisite for agility in system delivery, is the adoption of a Loosely Coupled approach.*

This approach provides an implementation paradigm, whereby systems can be developed and combined in a highly flexible way. This delivery agility will in turn drive overall organisational agility.

Any organisation that simply adopts *only* this approach, would immediately derive a significant step change in the way that they are able to implement and upgrade systems. This is because these modifications would be achievable, *without* significant disruption to any existing data flows.

> **Principle 120** *Agile organisations must be Loosely Coupled organisations.*

The fundamental principle of the Loosely Coupled paradigm, is to concentrate on the Data at Flow definitions, rather than the Data at Rest. This shift in emphasis makes a lot of sense given the increased focus on COTS products and Cloud based solutions. In most cases these obfuscate their Data at Rest structures behind interfaces.

It surprises me how many organisations still don't implement this Loosely Coupled model. And possibly even more surprising, is that many organisations that start to adopt, or have already adopted, this approach, still have not created the fundamental definitions required for its success.

With this in mind, let's look at how we need to create the architectural foundations so that we can drive real agility in delivery.

## Data Flow Diagrams

In order to be able to conceptualise and communicate the principles that underpin the Loosely Coupled design framework, we need a modelling syntax in addition to those already described.

A simple modelling syntax that can help to ensure the success of this approach, is the Data Flow Diagram (DFD).

Of particular importance, is the way that DFDs define system boundaries and identify any data that flows across them.

---

**Principle 121** *A Data Flow Diagram can provide significant value by documenting how proposed systems, and their data flows, will fit into the current data and system landscapes.*

---

Although DFDs have been used since the dawn of the data era, I still see many data flow models that ignore the importance of a well-defined system boundary.

Figure 59 is a real anonymised DFD that I saw a while ago.

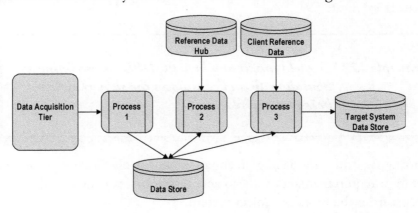

**Figure 59 – Data Flow Diagrams *without* system boundaries**

Comparing this with the model in figure 60, clearly demonstrates the power of a *simple* boundary in transforming understanding.

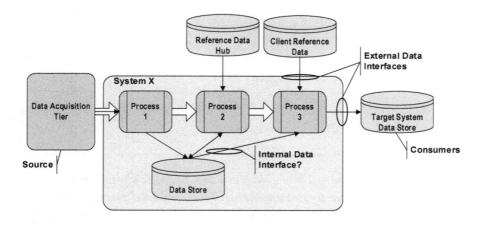

**Figure 60 – Data Flow Diagrams *with* system boundaries**

What the boundary brings into sharp relief, is exactly what is inside and what is outside the system being specified. Notice also that the syntax in figure 60, has separated the data flows from the process flows. This again reveals something of importance about the design approach, and has revealed aspects about the orchestration of the process flows, that were absent from figure 59.

> **Principle 122**   *To yield maximum benefit, DFDs must define a boundary that encapsulates the subject system being considered.*

Importantly, this modelling technique, not only identifies interface definition requirements, but it also acts to symbolically de-couple external systems from the model's subject system.

> **Principle 123**   *The symbolic de-coupling provided by DFDs, results in a clearer understanding of the design and implementation options available to ensure success.*

We shall return to this idea, once we understand a little more about how we implement the Loosely Coupled approach.

There are three levels at which Data Flow Diagrams are extremely powerful, these are when considering:

1. High-level System Context

2. System Tiers

3. Discrete Components

The importance of these is described below.

## High-level Context

A high-level DFD regards the system being modelled, as an abstracted high-level process. Creating this model type, helps to reveal *all* the systems and stakeholders involved, particularly all the data *sources* and all data *consumers*.

Importantly, the high-level Context model also defines the boundary for the proposed system. This boundary definition has many design and implementation implications that require careful assessment that we will see later in the book.

> **Principle 124  A high-level DFD should be considered as a mandatory artefact required during the initiation phase of any delivery work-stream.**

Of course, should subsequent phases modify the data flows of the subject system, then the DFD will naturally need to be updated.

At this macro level we can characterise these DFDs as defining systems or applications.

## System Tiers

DFDs are also extremely useful for defining the layers within system development. This is especially the case where there are multiple technical tiers within a stack, or where a complex system is being developed using combinations of distinct sub-components.

Looking at figure 60 again, we can see that, in this case, there are also *internal* interfaces suggested, between the data stores and processes 1, 2 and 3.

## Discrete Components

Discrete Components are those encapsulated system elements that operate without any dependency on any other part of the system landscape.

> **Principle 125** **Discrete Components have no knowledge of the implementation specifics of any other system or component, with which they are able to exchange data and events.**

We can only enable the Discrete Component concept through the adoption of a Loosely Coupled system landscape. But through its delivery, we are able to use a highly agile, 'plug and play' approach to add new components or: enhance, replace, or demise existing components.

At this micro level the DFDs can be directly applicable to defining part of the universe of Micro-services.

Although we have described three levels of DFDs, in fact we can think of them all as Discrete Components in our Loosely Coupled system landscape. Thus, we can use this single term to simplify the descriptions going forwards.

## Loosely Coupled Boundaries

The Discrete Component paradigm, necessitates the creation of well-defined boundaries. This relies upon constraining component interaction, through tightly-controlled interface definitions.

These interface definitions must define _contracts_ for data and event exchanges.

> **Principle 126** **Discrete Components need to be developed to only communicate with each other, using well defined Interface contracts.**

This simple idea is illustrated in figure 61.

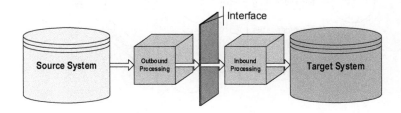

**Figure 61 – Discrete System boundaries**

## System Boundary Permeability

The Discrete Component boundaries must therefore be defined to _encapsulate_ their implementation specifics[44].

> **Principle 127** **Discrete System (boundary) interfaces must be permeable to data and events, but impermeable to any implementation specifics.**

As a very simple example, if naming conventions are technology, or system dependent, then these _must not_ cross the boundaries.

This however, immediately raises the question of what standards and definitions will be used at the interfaces _between_ all the components?

The answer to this question is revealed in the following section.

---

44    We will return to this design pattern when developing the Data Governance Framework Process definitions. These should also be Loosely Coupled and agnostic to the internal activities of each other.

## Interface Design For Discrete Components

What happens when we want to hook multiple Discrete Components together using our interface contract concept?

One approach is to create *specific* interfaces for each additional system that communicates with a target system. This scenario is represented in figure 62.

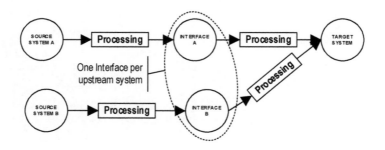

**Figure 62 – Unsustainable interface model**

As we add more and more data flows between Discrete Components though, this approach will result in a proliferation of specific interfaces, as illustrated in figure 62. Essentially, although we have interfaces, we are not Loosely Coupled, but tightly coupled!

Clearly this is not a sustainable pattern.

## Triangulation Principle

To achieve a more sustainable approach, we can borrow the Triangulation technique from currency exchanging. This is based upon the idea that we don't need to map every instance of currency to currency conversions. All we need to do, is choose a special standard currency and map each currency's exchange rate to that.

Figure 63 illustrates this principle, using the US Dollar as the standard or base currency.

| US Dollar versus | Rate | Inverse |
|---|---|---|
| Euro | 0.724860 | 1.379578 |
| Pound Sterling | 0.605901 | 1.650435 |
| ... | ... | ... |

**Figure 63 – Currency exchange rates**

From this set of conversions, we can calculate *any* required currency to currency conversion rate, by using their respective conversion rates to the *standard* currency. But how do we apply this idea to our interfaces?

## Interfaces And The Enterprise Data Models

The obvious choice for the common standard, is to align the interface specifications with the Enterprise Data Model's definitions. This, of course, is the job of the Canonical Model.

---

*Principle 128*    *In a Loosely Coupled system environment, the Canonical Data Model will drive interface definition conformance across the system landscape.*

---

This technique can be represented conceptually as in figure 64.

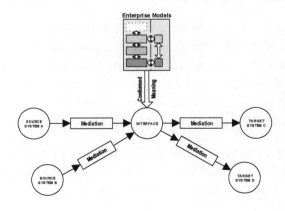

**Figure 64 – Sustainable interface model**

By using the Enterprise Canonical Model to provide a standard data transfer definition, we can achieve a sustainable approach which is:

- Target agnostic and

- Source agnostic

This will create the basis for implementing a successful Discrete Component approach that supports a 'plug and play' model.

The important role played by the Canonical Model to define the data structures and attribution, is shown in figure 65.

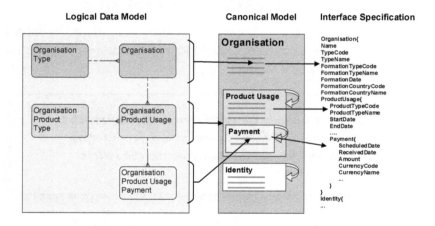

**Figure 65 – Conforming interface definitions with the Logical Data Model**

For the normalised data, it is clear in this schematic how the normalised Logical Data Model is the authority for the Canonical Model. But we also need to consider that when we transport aggregated or de-normalised data[45], we should still have a set of definitions for these that are conformed at an Enterprise level. This will allow us to transport data, such as 'Revenue Year To Date Amount', and be sure that this is consistent across all systems.

We must also remember the need for the Canonical Models to ensure conformance of the definitions above the individual Data at Flow 'protocols', for example, XSDs, or JSON/Avro.

---

45   Out of a de-normalised reporting hub as an example.

## Converging the System Landscape

As the Canonical Model patterns are repeatedly implemented, they create *convergence to* the Enterprise Data Models, and hence *align* the system landscape. This is illustrated schematically in figure 66.

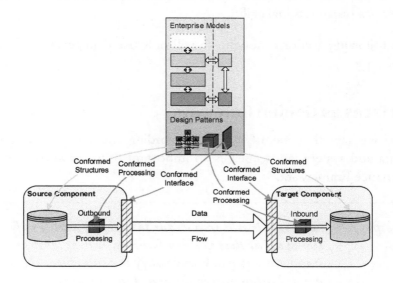

**Figure 66 – Enterprise Models driving conformance[46]**

We will pick up this theme again in the 'Organisational Agility' chapter, and see how we formalise it use.

## Read And Write Interfaces

Although we have described the benefits of interfaces using the data access examples, we should not forget that the data needs to get into our Data at Rest structures in the first place!

Again interfaces have to play a key role here. We will obscure the internal implementation through 'write methods' provided by formalised and agreed interfaces. We have to thank the Object Oriented era for the rapid evolution of this concept.

Today, the advent of Agile delivery means that the components need to be

---

46    Refer back to figure 35 on page 91, where this concept of using the Enterprise Data Models to drive the implementation patterns was first described.

scaled down to be more atomic. The requirement to mesh with Agile has also helped to drive the rapid ascendancy of the Micro-services paradigm. These atomic work-units of our system landscape, promote true system, and hence, organisational agility. In addition, by removing the duplication of processes and code-base components, they simultaneously transform delivery *and* organisational agility.

In the following sections though, we will only use data access to simplify the concepts.

## Interfaces as Golden Gateways

Earlier, we saw that identifying and recording the Golden Sources in our data and system landscapes, is an important foundation of our Data Governance Framework.

> *Principle 129*  *Whilst it is still important to identify and certify the Data at Rest Golden Sources, it is at least as important to track and ratify the interfaces that act as authoritative Data at Flow sources.*

This approach gives rise to the idea that interfaces should be ratified as Golden Gateways for data. That is, they need to be mandated as the only sources that can be used to consume data from, in all development activities.

Notice that in figure 67, a Golden Gateway can be the consumer of data from any combination of the following:

- one or more Golden Sources and/or

- one or more Golden Gateways

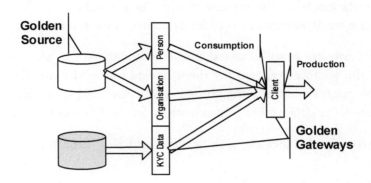

**Figure 67 – Golden Gateways and data flows**

## Ratifying Golden Gateways

Golden Gateways should be the *only* points of distribution of the data across our system landscapes. They can consume data from Data at Rest structures and/or other Gateways. Because of this, the ratification of the data they produce will depend on its authority level in the underlying source, either Golden Source or Golden Gateway. Notice that it must not only inherit the authority level of its source, but also the terms and conditions of the data source[47].

Therefore, *its* consumers will need to agree to the underlying sources conditions of use, plus any variations that the Gateway adds to these. For example, if it consumes data elements that have Data Privacy requirements, but does not produce these to its consumers, then the Data Privacy constraints can be removed from its consumers.

If there are any changes to the source's terms and conditions, then a Golden Gateway will also need to notify its consumers of these changes and seek their agreement.

## APIs And Other Interfaces

Application Program Interfaces (APIs) changed everything.

They came about to obscure the internals of systems from their

---

47    Please refer back to page 122 for a suggested list of these.

communication with the outside world. As a result, they allow flexible combinations of systems to seamlessly interoperate and exchange data.

The API concept is still retained, and even today people talk about APIs, despite the technology used for them having changed markedly over the years. We must remember though that strictly speaking they only represent one part of the data exchange mechanisms in the Loosely Coupled world.

These typically also include, Web Services and files — still!

## Interfaces and Data Lineage

APIs and their sibling interfaces, break the Point to Point Data Lineage model. In this world of interface based data flows, we only need to trace the *individual* Data Lineage steps of:

- *each* Source *to an* interface

- *each* Consumer *from an* interface

The sources and consumers using an interface can change rapidly, and this is one of the key benefits of Loose Coupling. But notice that we never actually need to track the end to end Data Lineage across the *entire* system landscape. If we ever need to know this picture, we can always build it by linking together the individual source to consumer 'stepping stones'.

In large organisations, the use of manual techniques to track the Data Lineage across their system landscape, is a tedious, error-prone, never-ending and resource intensive burden. Often remediation for compliance with regulations and legislation has forced this thankless task on organisations.

Fortunately, tools are increasingly becoming available that can 'auto-discover' sources and their consumers. In addition, they have features such as being able to profile the data passing between them. Adopting these tools will provide a real time analysis that all organisations would be wise to employ.

## Internal versus External Consumers

We must consider a subtle distinction in our consumers.

Not all access to our data structures will be from *external* actors. Where consumers are *within* the same 'application' for example, it seems overkill to create formal, ratified, externally-facing interfaces. Yet, we must apply the same good principles of Loosely Coupled components.

To describe this more clearly, let's look at an example in more detail. Over the years, I have worked on a number of work-streams where the mantra was one of 'vertical responsibility'. This approach meant that each Software Engineer was tasked with creating the application modules in an environment they were familiar with, e.g. Java or .NET. Beyond this though, they were expected to develop the corresponding database modules, to execute queries and DML in the database.

Often though, their understanding of database techniques was basic, and SQL optimisation skills rudimentary. In addition, their understanding of the application Business and Data Rules was sketchy at best. Naturally enough, the productivity and maintainability of what was developed, was often compromised by these constraints.

We can consider their database modules as *internal* consumers[48]. We could not seriously suggest that creating RESTful APIs to de-couple the database data structures from the database modules, is a good pattern. Yet, we still need to consider the possibility of creating an interface of some sort.

Using my involvement in these work-streams, I changed the approach. I created a comprehensive set of database Interface Layer Entities and Methods, and then assisted each Software Engineer to find the appropriate of these for their requirements.

The relief was palpable.

Often the Software Engineers would say phrases such as 'Is that all I need to do?'

Compared with the previous approach[49], it seemed amazing to them that all they now had to do, for example, was choose the attributes they required from an appropriate existing Interface Layer Entity.

---

48   Look again at figure 60 to see the Internal Interface hint.
49   Adopting a Micro-services approach would have alleviated some of these problems, but not all!

In addition, the Interface Layer Entities had aspects such as data entitlements and 'pseudo deletion filtering', already built into their definition. This again removed the need for each Software Engineer to build such capabilities into their own components, leading to extremely rapid development and robust deliveries.

There was a profound improvement in productivity and, in addition, there was a dramatic *slump* in the number of database related defects.

## Interfaces Beyond Interoperability

In a Loosely Coupled system landscape, insulating our data transport from the internals of our Data at Rest structures, provides many positive benefits. Discrete component interoperability is the absolutely fundamental of these. But there are many others.

If implemented correctly, these will cumulatively add to the organisation's true delivery agility. But before we see the benefits, it makes sense to remind ourselves of the problem.

In the absence of a Loosely Coupled approach, each individual 'point solution' consumer can have an interpretation of the data that varies, at least to some degree, from the others. Figure 68 illustrates the problem of multiple consumers making direct access to the internal data structures.

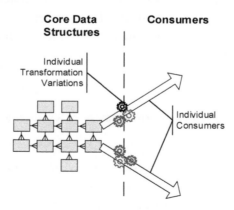

**Figure 68 – Non-conformed 'point solution' consumer access**

Each interpretation requires an understanding of the data for its construction, and each uses custom built interpretations that are:

- costly

- error prone

- buried in the code-base

- not insulated against changes of the data structures

Interoperability demands the use of ratified interfaces, but as we saw in the previous section, *internal* consumers are not necessarily best served by *external* interfaces.

However, it still makes a lot of sense to create an Interface Layer to decouple access.

Looking at figure 69, we can see that because the meaning of our data is instantiated in an Interface Layer, all the consumer calls have become *very* simple.

Each inherits the benefits from the *conformance* of the data's interpretation.

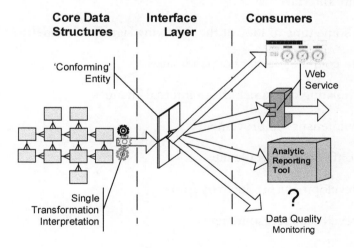

**Figure 69 – Conformed Interface Layer**

This simplification of access for the multiple and constantly changing consumers, is where the real cost and productivity benefits are delivered.

> **Principle 130** **Creating a well-designed Interface Layer for data access, can provide a dramatic improvement in delivery, maintenance costs and also defect reduction.**

In figure 69, notice the use of an externally facing interface. This Web Service, in common with the Application consumers, makes use of the same Interface Layer Entity.

What this schematic illustrates is that our Interface Layer can actually be any combination of:

- Internal Layer
- External Interface

To simplify the descriptions of the *concept* going forwards, we will simply consider an 'Interface Layer'.

Let's take some time to look at the following significant benefits:

- De-coupling delivery dependencies
- Insulating consumers from internal changes
- Maintenance improvement
- Conformed Data Quality
- Development productivity gains
- Development resourcing
- Physical model re-factoring
- Incremental adoption
- Business and Data Rule visibility

These are described in more detail in the following sections.

## De-coupling Delivery Dependencies

De-coupling the Discrete Component being considered for delivery, from dependencies on external Discrete Components, provides an extremely powerful benefit. These de-coupled dependencies, can either be during the Discrete Component development, or even at deployment. For example, we can use a range of techniques to provide a tactical source, or stub an external system that is itself under development. Once the strategic solution is available to be deployed, it can be used to replace the tactical.

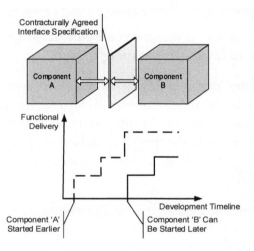

**Figure 70 – De-coupling development using Loose Coupling**

In figure 70, we see that as a result of agreeing a contract signature between two Discrete Components that are being developed, both can proceed with their internal development, confident of their interoperability when they are completed.

> ***Principle 131  An agreed Interface Layer enables concurrent development of multiple interacting Discrete Components.***

## Insulating Consumers from Internal Changes

Whereas the previous advantage relates to delivery, this advantage allows enhancements to proceed without any dependencies. This is possible, because data can only be exchanged through defined interfaces, and therefore any internal details are obscured.

> **Principle 132** **Discrete Component delivery agility, can be dramatically improved, by insulating data consumers from any modifications to the internal data implementation details.**

The caveat here though, is that the changed Data at Rest implementation, must still be able to honour any existing *contract*/$s^{50}$.

In terms of agility, this is a crucial advantage delivered by the Loosely Coupled approach. It allows individual systems to be modified, with negligible disruption to any of the other systems with which they exchange data or events. As a result, the overall organisation system agility is radically improved. And, as we know, improved system agility, equals improved organisation delivery

It also tells us something else that is vitally important and stated in principle 133.

> **Principle 133** **In a Loosely Coupled world, the internal representation of 'Data at Rest', is not nearly as important as it used to be in the Point to Point world.**

As a result, the emphasis we used to place upon governing the Physical Data Models for implemented systems, is not nearly as critical as it was.

## Maintenance Improvement

In the absence of an Interface Layer, enhancements or bug-fixes to a system may be costly and difficult to deliver.

---

50   However, there is some ability to upgrade or deprecate interface specifications - with agreement of the existing consumers!

Finding all the parts of the code-base that implemented a particular interpretation of the data structures, becomes a significant problem. This is because each Software Engineer has been free to solve the data requirements in the way that occurs to them at the time. As a result, each code statement is likely to be at least slightly different.

At the end of this search to unearth the candidates for change, the potentially difficult modifications to this code needs to be carried out.

This work is often made more problematic because, since the component was first delivered, the legacy software expertise has been lost from the organisation. As a result, the changes become a slow, and error-prone hard slog.

Of course, all the changes will, need to be thoroughly tested. But, due to the sheer volume of these, this can also cause a considerable strain on resources.

By contrast, with a defined Interface Layer, the search for data access code becomes much easier. This is simply because there are orders of magnitude, fewer data access code points. Once the areas for change are identified, the amount of code that needs to be changed is significantly less, and as a result, the testing effort will also be radically reduced.

## Conformed Data Quality

Data Quality is a pre-requisite for maximising the benefit an organisation can derive from its data. Of course, if we carry out the Data Quality checking at the Interface Layer, the vast majority of the Data Quality issues will be fixed for *all* of its data consumers. Thus, as a result of the adopting an Interface Layer, we will increase the Data Quality for all consumers. Simultaneously we will reduce the effort and latency required for Data Quality fixes.

There will, of course, be additional checks required within each set of consumer specific access, as these will have undertaken various transformations of the data from the Interface Layer. But, these activities would still be needed, with or without, the Interface Layer.

Therefore, the gains in overall Data Quality, and significant reduction of

Data Quality fixes, will have a dramatic transformation in this key area of our Data Governance.

## Development Productivity Gains

The following chart indicates the benefits delivered by making the relatively small effort to design and develop an Interface Layer.

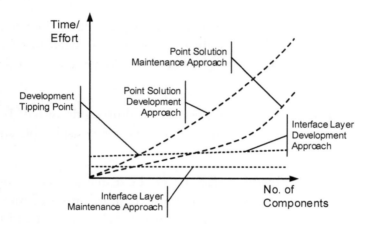

**Figure 71 – Development cost comparison of an Interface Layer**

What figure 71 illustrates, is the cost of developing data access code as point solutions, compared with developing an Interface Layer. But reassuringly, in a delivery work-stream you do not need to slot in several *extra* months to develop such a layer. On the contrary, figure 71 illustrates that the benefits should outweigh the costs *almost* immediately.

Notice that there is a point below which, an Interface Layer does not justify its construction purely based on the productivity gains alone. But, I would strongly argue that it still makes sense to create one for all of the other key reasons listed in this chapter.

## Development Resourcing Impacts

Often delivery is hampered by a lack of highly skilled Software Engineers who *also* have a good knowledge of the organisation's operations and Business and Data Rules. Partly, as described before, the scarcity of SMEs' time is often also a major impediment. In addition, any dislocations in the IT and Business realms can lead to a lack of true commitment and communication between these critical functions. As a result, the transfer of data IP to delivery teams is often less than perfect.

These constraints can be further exacerbated in situations where the code-base development is:

1. Out-sourced and/or

2. Off-shore

3. Globally dispersed

The Interface Layer can be extremely beneficial in these circumstances. This is because, to develop it, is a relatively low cost activity that can be used to encapsulate complex, operational understanding and Business and Data Rules.

A further organisational benefit is that the SME input is reduced to pretty much a single call on their expertise during the construction of the layer. As a result their commitment is fresh, and they do not become weary of explaining the same details, *yet again with another team.*

---

**Principle 134   An Interface Layer approach allows relatively few,**
**highly skilled in-house resources to encapsulate**
**operational, Business and Data Rules.**

---

The resulting highly performant layer and feature-rich Interface Layer, can then be leveraged by relatively low skilled (and cost) resources. This approach removes the need for these consumer resources to understand *any* of the transformation complexity that has been built into the layer. Instead, they can concentrate in the areas where their expertise is strongest, that is, the consuming software features and the delivery requirements of the data.

This is illustrated in figure 72, which shows that the required level of data source technology and Business and Data Rule expertise, is very low for the externally developed consumer code.

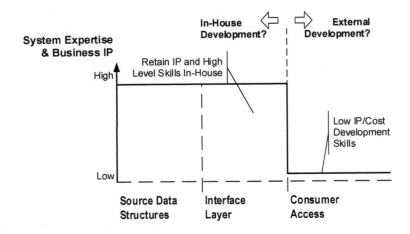

Figure 72 – Interface Layer development impact

We can see clearly how an Interface Layer helps mitigate the negative impacts of the delivery resourcing models that are currently prevalent.

> **Principle 135** *An Interface Layer helps to mitigate the negative impact of consumer development by not requiring the consumer delivery team to have: Source data technical expertise, or detailed Business Rule or Data Rule knowledge.*

## Physical Model Re-factoring

We've considered many advantages offered by the Interface Layer, but there is one that is almost totally ignored, and yet is extremely powerful. This is based upon the ability of the Interface Layer Entities to re-interpret underlying Physical Data Structures. The problems that this can solve are particularly relevant where the sources are COTS products, or were engineered without conformance with the Enterprise Data Models. We can use this technique to effectively retro-fit such understanding onto these sources.

As a simple example, let's consider a Super Type which is represented in the physical database by more than one table. Imagine that a Party Super Type is physicalised in the database as separate tables, containing Individuals and Organisation data.

A single Interface Layer Entity can be constructed across these, to represent the Super Type Entity, as illustrated in figure 73.

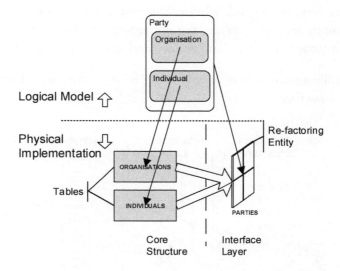

**Figure 73 – Interface Layer Entities re-factoring physical implementations[51]**

---

***Principle 136*** ***Interface Layer Entities can be used to re-factor structures to for example, conform to Enterprise definitions, without needing to re-factor the underlying data structures.***

---

We can see immediately that consumers interested in obtaining a consolidated picture of the Parties, now have a single source. Without this Entity, they would need to determine how to combine the data from the underlying data structures.

## Incremental Adoption

It isn't always possible to deliver an Interface Layer into the system landscape using a single big bang. This is highly likely to be the case when retrofitting one to a live system.

---

51   For clarity the Physical Data Model layer, between the Logical Data Model and Physical Implementation layer, is not included in this diagram.

However, it is possible to adopt an incremental approach that will allow the layer to be gradually implemented as opportunities arise. These opportunities typically occur when consumer systems need enhancements or requires fixes or, indeed, wholesale replacement. At the same time that these changes are being made, the consumer can be weaned off the old direct data structure access, and re-factored to use the new Interface Layer.

Figure 74 illustrates how consumers can be incrementally weaned off the core data structures.

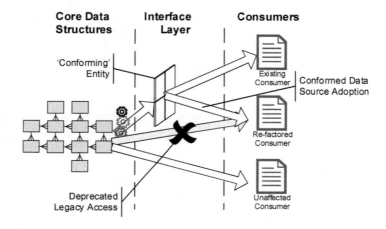

**Figure 74 – Interface Layer incremental adoption**

What this schematic illustrates is that new consumers can be based upon the Interface Layer, and as the opportunity arises, existing consumers can be re-factored to make use of these Entities. This approach allows existing consumers to continue to use the old access without any immediate requirement to use the new structures.

In the past, when I have been involved in such re-factoring activities the simplification of the code-base has demonstrated a dramatic confirmation of the Interface Layer approach.

## Business and Data Rule Visibility

In the absence of an Interface Layer approach to development, the interpretation of the underlying data structures often becomes buried in the code-base.

As a result, in order to understand and validate these interpretations, requires resources to *reverse engineer* the code. This can be an extremely costly exercise that requires significant time and resources.

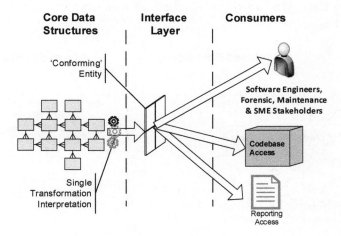

**Figure 75 – Shared visibility of source data**

An Interface Layer can remove this constraint, by providing simple data access that is consistent for all consumers. An example of the advantages are that this produces, is the dramatically improved 'time to resolution' of consumer related data issues.

This, in turn, leads to a Discrete Component with significantly reduced maintenance costs and improved agility.

---

*Principle 137  An Interface Layer can be used to provide shared access and understanding of the data by a wide group of consumers and stakeholders.*

---

## Micro-services

We cannot leave this chapter without some words about Micro-services. Whilst there is not the space in this book to get to the detail of Micro-service architecture, we should highlight some of the aspects that Data Architecture needs to consider.

Micro-service development carves up the operational functional universe illustrated in figure 17 on page 41 into discrete components. Each of one represents the smallest coherent set of operational function and its supporting data. We can think of them as the atomic work-units of our Data Landscape.

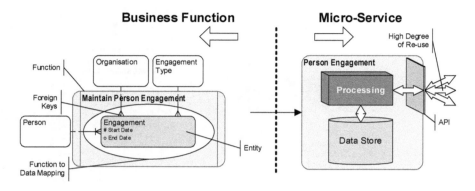

**Figure 76 – Atomic Business Function to Micro-service**

The Micro-services approach to development fully exploits all of the advantages called out in this chapter.

Each Micro-service has complete domain over a discrete set of supporting data structures. Often this is characterised as being a separate data store but actually this may be too much of a simplification. For example Data Hosting rules may dictate that a global organisation would require many separately hosted micro-databases per Micro-service. As with all design decisions there will be a trade-off; in this case minimising the moving parts with pure separation of concerns.

Figure 77 illustrates a powerful advantage provided by Micro-services and that is the concept of Separation of Concerns. Notice that the 'database' in this schematic is virtual.

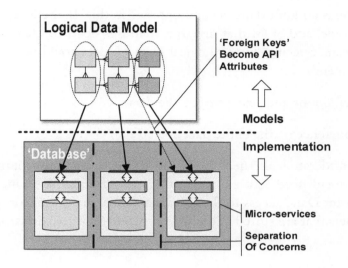

**Figure 77 – Micro-service and separation of concerns**

We *could* implement it in a single database instance, or multiple. This is because the physical structures are isolated from each other. To be clear; there is no requirement to build the entire set of structures as a single conformed dataset as in a Relational Database implementation.

Immediately we can see many advantages to this approach. For example, it supports a heterogeneous deployment landscape such as Cloud versus On-Premise based upon the datasets.

The success of this delivery strategy relies to a great part on well thought through Standard Operating Models and their documented data usage of the Logical Data Model Entities and Attributes. Not only does the entire universe of functions need to be accurately defined, but their decomposition into the atomic Functions also needs to be agreed with all stakeholders *before* the Micro-service design can proceed.

But as with the Logical Data Model development, we can start with discrete functional areas as long as the entire high-level universe has been specified. This will ensure coherence for what is delivered, whilst at the same time facilitating an incremental approach that meshes well with an agile organisation.

The accuracy of SOM definitions is always key here. However, the Logical

Data Model is an important 'second opinion' in this. If there are areas of the data model and SOM that disagree, then this helps to Quality Assure both of them. Specifically, the Logical Data Model should be used as an authority to enforce:

- Definitions and structures of the data

- Coherence of the entire data universe

Careful consideration also needs to be given to how common controls over the data are enforced across a suite of Micro-services. These include: its use of Master Data, access to the data, 'referential integrity'[52], or querying large datasets that are stored in multiple different 'isolated' datastores.

---

52  Ensuring shared keys across a complex heterogeneous landscape can be problematic!

# 8: Organisational Agility

*Only those organisations that are innately agile, will survive and thrive into the future.*

The challenges for organisations rain down at an ever accelerating rate and with constantly increasing complexity.

For an organisation to survive and thrive within this environment, it must be able to respond to change ever more rapidly.

This predicts that the only organisations that will make it through the next decade are those that are *intrinsically agile*. Since almost all organisations rely on systematised data, this requirement dictates that they are able to rapidly change their system landscape.

> **Principle 138   Organisational Agility is ever more dependent on System Agility.**

But the real challenge, is to make rapid changes without losing the benefit from their key enabling resource - their data. Therefore, the response must be made with a sure-footed foundation that guarantees a sustainable future.

Consequently, we must use governance processes to assure any changes. The conundrum to solve is, how to *enforce governance* whilst *enabling agility*.

In the view of most work-streams, instruments such as Data Governance, have at best, *obstructed* their delivery.

But in the last chapter, we started to realise that actually Data Architecture has the potential to *radically boost* the agility of our organisations. This is achieved by bringing good Data Architecture directly to the code-face of delivery.

This book uses Data Governance as the lens through which we can describe how to implement this boost to agility. A benefit of doing this, is that trail-blazing these patterns through Data Governance is an easy story to sell to organisations. This is because for many of them, they are unable to function, unless they are able to demonstrate compliance of their data and policies, with external regulatory and/or legislative regimes. As a result, their key stakeholders, will be acutely pre-disposed to the approach promoted by this book.

In this chapter, we will describe how we can mesh development *and* Data Governance, so that each works to amplify the benefits from the other.

As a result, their integration will provide the organisation with *true agility*, and at the same time, *guaranteed sustainability*.

## Opening The Flood Gates

The biggest worries for those charged with the oversight of delivery within an organisation, are around the system fragmentation and potential loss of regulatory, legislative compliance and/or reputation.

> *Principle 139   The loss of effective Data Governance over delivery, can cause breaches of regulatory, legislative compliance or reputational loss.*

In the past, a typical approach to avoid these consequences has been the interception of delivery at key points, using Data Governance and Architectural Review 'Gate' processes. These have been intended to check if the development is, 'still on track', and has 'done the right thing'.

In my view, these Gate processes have always been an ineffective, and often, a negative, blunt instrument. They have typically intercepted far too late in the delivery process, and as a result, created waste by triggering the following painful 'adjustments' to what has been delivered:

- Re-stating – describing what has been done in 'palatable' terms

- Re-positioning – shifting the delivery to fit review criteria

- Re-working – hasty redevelopment to tweak what has been delivered

All of these activities take effort, and cause the delivery teams to 'take their eyes off the ball', resulting in a loss of momentum. The approach proposed in this book promises to remove such Gate processes.

But if the Gates are removed, how will we ensure good Architecture still prevails, and also be assured of compliance, and all the other benefits that they were intended to guarantee?

The challenge for an Agile Organisation is to guarantee that these benefits are not lost.

## Symbiosis Between Architecture And Delivery

Enterprise Architecture is often viewed as imposing impediments to delivery. This viewpoint holds that; the more control an organisation imposes over delivery, the less agile its delivery becomes.

In other words, good delivery and good Architecture are intrinsically at loggerheads, as illustrated in figure 78.

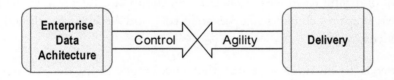

**Figure 78 – Architecture *versus* Delivery**

This logic suggests that to be able to develop more stuff, more quickly, any Architectural input must be removed. But actually, as we have seen in the chapter on 'Architectural Agility', this reasoning is absolutely false.

Instead, we need to use the benefits of each one, to boost the benefits from the other, as indicated in figure 79.

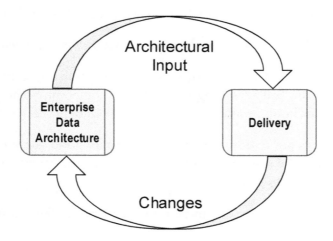

**Figure 79 – Virtuous circle between Architecture and Delivery**

If we can achieve the virtuous circle as in figure 79, then we will be able to create the mutually beneficial relationships that align the functions across our organisations, as illustrated in figure 38 on page 99.

So let's find out how to make this a practical reality.

## Injecting Architecture Into Delivery

Instead of trying to squeeze deliveries through Gate Reviews, in my mind the correct approach has *always been* to inject good Architecture directly into the delivery *up front*.

This needs to be done in a way that encourages Software Engineers to adopt it as 'the path of least resistance'.

> *Principle 140  A far better way than using Gate Reviews to assure delivery processes, is to inject the 'goodness' directly into them.*

We will use two major mechanisms to enable successful injection of Data Architectural goodness into development, and they are:

1. A source of sound Data Architectural patterns

2. Skills and information transfer from SMEs

Figure 80 illustrates these two dissemination mechanisms injecting good Data Architecture directly into delivery activities.

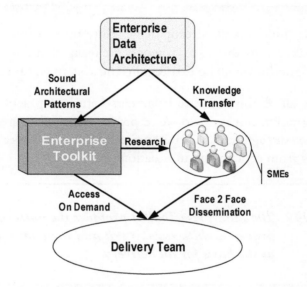

**Figure 80 – Injection of Architectural patterns *into* Delivery**

This schematic describes the essence of our approach which is described in more detail in the following sections.

## The Enterprise Toolkit

A key theme of this book is the provision of an Enterprise Toolkit. This will contain patterns and components that will be used as the building blocks that the Software Engineers will adopt, adapt and 'snap together' to create innovative solutions.

If we think of system component delivery as an exam, we can think of the Enterprise Toolkit as providing specimen answers for all of the questions.

> **Principle 141** *The Enterprise Toolkit will contain best-practice 'specimen answers' to the 'questions' posed by requirement specifications to the delivery teams.*

The building blocks will already have Enterprise Data Architectural goodness 'baked into them', and hence, by using them as the basis for delivery, this goodness will be carried into the system environment.

By providing all of the Software Engineers with best-practice patterns as their starting point, not only do we improve what is delivered, but at the same time we *boost* agility. This is because each Engineer is not left to figure out solutions from scratch and in isolation[53].

> **Principle 142** *The Enterprise Toolkit provides the patterns of proven architectural merit and these must be used as the basis for all delivery.*

This approach will give the organisation the agility to deliver components characterised by innovation, but simultaneously, they will drive conformance, by adopting optimal architectural patterns.

> **Principle 143** *The Enterprise Toolkit will enforce good Data Governance and, at the same time, boost delivery agility.*

These patterns should, at a minimum, include:

- Data and Process Models

- Implementation Patterns

---

53    Refer back to figure 35 on page 91, to see the role of the Enterprise Data Models in this.

- Data Quality profiles

- Testing Patterns

- Standards, Guidelines and Policy definitions

- Training material

- Internal and External references

Some core elements to consider, are shown schematically in figure 81.

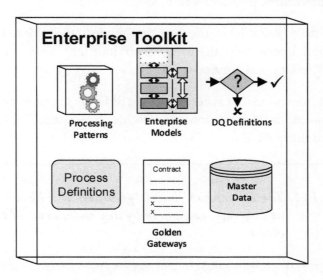

**Figure 81 – The Enterprise Toolkit**

Although this book is primarily concerned with Data Architecture, the same approach has a wider applicability than this. Cyber-security, or automated masking of production data for non-production environments, are examples of the wider types of patterns that the Enterprise Toolkit should also incorporate.

## Enforcing Data Governance

We can think of Data Governance as the effective implementation of Enterprise Data Architecture 'on the ground'. Thus, we can see that by injecting the patterns sourced from the Toolkit directly into the system landscape, we will also inject the foundations of Data Governance alongside them. But, we still need to describe the processes that will fully integrate and guarantee this approach.

## The 24x7 Self-Service Store

One way we can think about the Enterprise Toolkit, is as a knowledge-base. But we also need to ensure that it is an *active dissemination component*. It must be designed and implemented to provide a firm basis for development for *its* consumers. Thus it must contain elements such as: on-demand training, interactive interfaces, podcasts and videos.

I have also used 'wizards' in the past that guide stakeholders through the processes and hence help them 'on their journey'. This simple feature makes the Toolkit a self-service store.

In chapter 1, we stated that access to scarce SMEs is a serious constraint for many organisations. We can now see how the Enterprise Toolkit can help to overcome this problem.

> *Principle 144*  *The Enterprise Toolkit 'goodness' can be accessed at anytime, anywhere by any team around the globe.*

## SME Skill Dissemination

In addition to the Enterprise Toolkit, we need to provide access to SMEs. No matter how good the training materials in the Enterprise Toolkit are, there will always be the need to coach people 'face to face' – even if this is only virtually! The SMEs will provide a second and more interactive, dissemination mechanism.

SMEs will themselves need to be familiar and up-to-date with their understanding of the Enterprise Toolkit patterns. This will ensure they are ideally positioned to help Software Engineers and others, to assimilate these patterns.

> **Principle 145** *In part, the SMEs' expertise needs to be derived from the Enterprise Toolkit.*

In addition, the SMEs will be required to help upskill the Software Engineers, and/or help in the selection of the correct components and patterns to use. They may also coach Software Engineers by co-developing components, assisting them to get 'up to speed' with previously unfamiliar patterns.

> **Principle 146** *The upskilling function of SMEs, provides an active, and effective feed-forward dissemination of the patterns contained in the Enterprise Toolkit.*

But, as we shall see later, there will need to be processes that will also drive the evolution of the Enterprise Toolkit patterns.

Before we can understand the way that we can use our two mechanisms to deliver good architecture, let's remind ourselves of the two major delivery paradigms and highlight the features that we will need as integration touchpoints.

## SDLC – Waterfall Overview

Before Agile, the predominant delivery methodology was called the Software Development Life Cycle (SDLC) - also widely known as Waterfall.

These days it has become largely discredited and out of vogue. This is due to a widespread belief that it has intrinsic flaws and that these have often led to partial, or total failure to deliver[54].

---

54   I have personally witnessed many dozens of SDLC developments, none of which failed. Indeed, *all* of them delivered systems that met or exceeded expectations.

SDLC is typically described as incorporating the following well-defined phases:

1. Analysis – specifying Requirements

2. Design – defining the Solution

3. Development – creating Solution infrastructure

4. Testing – ensuring the developed Solution meets the Requirements

5. Deployment – implementing the Solution

Figure 82 illustrates the usual representation of Waterfall and shows why this tag became associated with it.

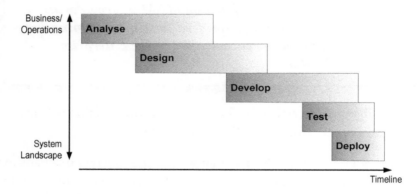

**Figure 82 – The Waterfall phases**

## The Truth about 'Monolithic' Waterfall

The Agilistas often characterise Waterfall as being *monolithic*. They suggest that as a result, it is intrinsically prone to systemic failures. However, although SDLC is often characterised as being monolithic, is this really true?

According to many, most of the programmes and projects, in the great graveyard of failed system deliveries, used SDLC. But, although this is probably true, what is not quite so clear, is that these failures can be directly attributed to the methodology itself.

In my experience the depiction of Waterfall as monolithic is actually a myth.

I am sure in some cases it *is* true, but I have *never* been on a Waterfall project where it was actually true. Where in figure 82 we can see a limited degree of phase overlap, in my experience good Project Managers and Delivery Teams are able to parallelise tasks in a much more granular fashion.

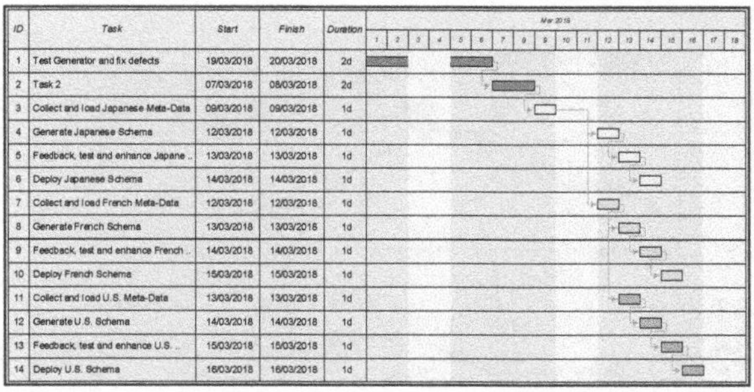

| ID | Task | Start | Finish | Duration | Mar 2018 |
|----|------|-------|--------|----------|----------|
| 1 | Test Generator and fix defects | 19/03/2018 | 20/03/2018 | 2d | |
| 2 | Task 2 | 07/03/2018 | 08/03/2018 | 2d | |
| 3 | Collect and load Japanese Meta-Data | 09/03/2018 | 09/03/2018 | 1d | |
| 4 | Generate Japanese Schema | 12/03/2018 | 12/03/2018 | 1d | |
| 5 | Feedback, test and enhance Japane .. | 13/03/2018 | 13/03/2018 | 1d | |
| 6 | Deploy Japanese Schema | 14/03/2018 | 14/03/2018 | 1d | |
| 7 | Collect and load French Meta-Data | 12/03/2018 | 12/03/2018 | 1d | |
| 8 | Generate French Schema | 13/03/2018 | 13/03/2018 | 1d | |
| 9 | Feedback, test and enhance French .. | 14/03/2018 | 14/03/2018 | 1d | |
| 10 | Deploy French Schema | 15/03/2018 | 15/03/2018 | 1d | |
| 11 | Collect and load U.S. Meta-Data | 13/03/2018 | 13/03/2018 | 1d | |
| 12 | Generate U.S. Schema | 14/03/2018 | 14/03/2018 | 1d | |
| 13 | Feedback, test and enhance U.S. .. | 15/03/2018 | 15/03/2018 | 1d | |
| 14 | Deploy U.S. Schema | 16/03/2018 | 16/03/2018 | 1d | |

**Figure 83 – The reality of monolithic SDLC**

In figure 83, we clearly can see a repeating pattern of Analysis, Design, Development and Deployment that are effectively mini-Waterfalls within Waterfalls. These are very similar to Agile Sprints but there is an inherent flexibility in the approach. For example, they are not necessarily time-boxed to uniform start and end dates. In addition they can bring a differing range of expertise to bear on problems in an extremely flexible manner. As a result there is far greater flexibility over what tasks are completed within any timeframe.

# The Agile Themes and Approach

The champions for Agile and DevOps, proclaim a fresh approach to development that will re-invigorate IT delivery.

Their mantra has several major themes:

- Smaller discrete deliveries ⇨ delivering benefits earlier, and responding earlier to feedback

- Co-location ⇨ better communication, improving quality and 'fit' to business needs

- Constant feedback ⇨ continually improving activities and deliverables

- Continual learning ⇨ cross-skilling, and keeping skills fresh

- Removal of waste ⇨ delivering benefits earlier, and more efficiently

Figure 84 shows the Agile and DevOps approach schematically.

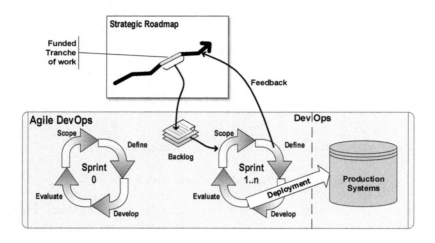

**Figure 84 – The Agile and DevOps approach**

## Sprints versus Mini-Waterfalls

If we look at Agile Sprints, unsurprisingly they contain many of the same features as are contained in SDLC Waterfall projects. Of course, there are significant differences. The Sprints are time-boxed, the teams are more self-contained and their members should remain (remarkably) permanent.

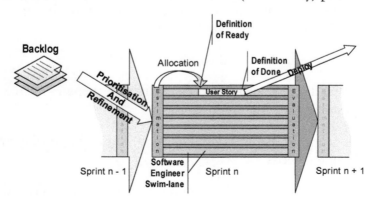

**Figure 85 – Timeboxed Agile DevOps Sprints**

Looking at figure 85, we can clearly see that Sprints require very similar activities to the mini-Waterfalls depicted in figure 83. This provides an opportunity to ensure that the way we integrate Data Architecture, should be as easy for SDLC as Agile DevOps Work-streams.

## Marrying Delivery To Requirements

The world that organisations face, presents a complex and ever-shifting set of constraints and opportunities. Within the realm of system delivery, the rate of technological change is accelerating every day, with each facet fragmenting with an unprecedented pace.

Even if in the past, organisations were able to ignore the failures of system delivery, they can no longer afford to do so. They simply cannot wait several years for a major system development, or transformation to be delivered. This is especially true, when what *is* delivered, is no longer relevant for the challenges being faced at the time of delivery.

This latter point leads to one advantage offered by Agile that, although rarely mentioned, overcomes a major flaw of the 'monolithic' approach of SDLC.

---

**Principle 147  With SDLC, if you can't afford the whole proposed development, you end up with nothing!**

---

This 'all or nothing' dichotomy has been quite debilitating for some organisations. As budgets have been squeezed, and demands have grown apace – they have often been left stranded, unable to deliver anything!

What figure 86 illustrates, is another key outcome that makes Agile potentially a far more effective contemporary approach than SDLC development.

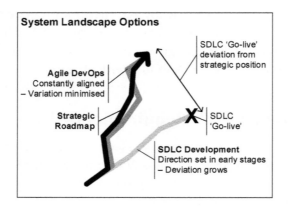

**Figure 86 – Agile – continually aligned**

Figure 86, compares two hypothetical 'parallel-universe' approaches to track a shifting Strategic direction; one using SDLC, the other Agile. The black arrow, represents the way that the direction of the Organisational Strategy, has constantly changed over time, across the possible range of system landscape options.

Looking at the light grey SDLC line, at the time that the development was started, it was well aligned with the Strategic direction. However, over time this original direction has looked increasingly irrelevant. The Strategy has moved on, but the SDLC development continued in the original direction, oblivious to these changes.

By contrast, the equivalent Agile development, continuously tracked the changes in the Strategic Roadmap, and as a result, it was able to minimise its deviation at all points[55].

> **Principle 148** *The mantra of system development in the future must be; 'little, often and constantly revise'.*

This gives us a clear visualisation of why major Projects or Programmes *can* end up being cancelled, or just scrapped upon delivery!

---

55  We can also see that the Micro-services approach on page 173 is an ideal approach for minimising the system landscape deviation from the strategic direction as per figure 86.

# Integrating De-coupled Processes

The processes of Data Governance are very different from those of delivery. And yet we must make them mesh.

In the preceding chapter, we discovered that an advantage of Discrete Components, is that they are agnostic to the internal processing of any other Discrete Components that they interact with. We will adopt an analogous approach for the integration of the Data Governance and the delivery processes.

In the system world, we use interfaces to define the signature for data exchange. In order to integrate Data Governance processes, we will define trigger points and specified payloads of meta-data that will be transferred to the triggered processes.

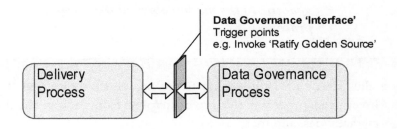

**Figure 87 – Data Governance trigger interface**

De-coupling not only provides insulation from any re-factoring of the processes on either side, but we *must use it*, to overcome a number of structural integration issues that arise from the two groups of processes.

These arise because, the Data Governance processes:

1. must be agnostic to any triggering methodology

2. have different Stakeholders, mechanisms and cadences from delivery

3. have timelines that are not necessarily contemporary

These factors are described in more detail in the following sections.

## Integration Must Be Methodology Agnostic

The Data Governance processes must be defined to be agnostic to the methodologies that trigger them. We need to ensure they work the same way irrespective of any flavour of delivery, for example:

- Agile+DevOps

- SDLC

- Data Migrations

- System de-commissioning

---

***Principle 149*** ***The Data Governance processes must be totally agnostic to the methodology of the triggering processes.***

---

This is illustrated at a high-level in figure 88, which shows that the same Data Governance processes, need to be invoked from each of the different triggering activities, and methodologies.

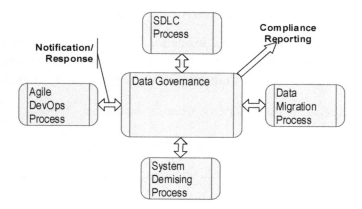

**Figure 88 – Data Governance processes must be trigger-process agnostic**

As an example, imagine regulatory compliance. It is quite obvious that to be able to demonstrate compliance to *external* regulators, we require the same evidence, *irrespective* of our *internal* delivery mechanisms.

## The Stakeholders, Mechanisms and Process Cadences are Different

We have already seen the need to ensure that Data Governance processes do not impede those of delivery. Due to their nature, the Data Governance processes typically have a longer time to completion than those required by the delivery cadence – especially two week Sprints.

> *Principle 150  Data Governance Processes will typically have a slower tempo than those of delivery, and so must be de-coupled from them.*

What we must not do, is introduce 'idle time' for the Software Engineers, whilst the Data Governance processes grind away. Therefore, it is unlikely that any but highly automated 'your notification has been received' type responses, could be immediately returned by Data Governance processes.

### Stakeholders Differ

By contrast to Data Governance, the key stakeholders in the delivery teams, are focussed on each individual delivery. As a result, they rarely take account of the overall Enterprise objectives. Additionally, because their roles are very different, their knowledge and skill sets will also be very different.

> *Principle 151  Data Governance processes will have very different stakeholders from the delivery activities, and so must be de-coupled from them.*

Notice that since we integrate the two sets of processes in a Loosely Coupled way, we also shield the Software Engineers from having to understand *any* of the implementation minutiae of the Data Governance processes[56].

---

56    See page 152, where each system must be oblivious of the inner workings of any other in a Loosely Coupled landscape.

## Mechanisms Differ

In the world of delivery, the mantra of automation and software integration is paramount. This emphasis helps to reduce waste and speed delivery.

By contrast, the processes of change in the Data Governance landscape, are people-driven to a far greater extent. Meetings and adjudication sessions, are much more prevalent in this world. Thought and judgement are brought to bear on issues, and if done well, these often take time[57].

---

**Principle 152  Data Governance will typically have different process mechanisms from those of delivery, and so must be de-coupled from them.**

---

# Designing The Data Governance Processes

This book cannot define the specific Data Governance processes for your organisation. But here is a suggested approach to the overall process:

1.  Define the process universe

2.  Use a centre of the universe focus

3.  Start with the Enterprise Data Models

Let's look at this approach in more detail.

## Define the Process Universe

When designing the Data Governance processes, always make sure these are *atomic*. This approach will provide the low-level granularity that we require to be able to invoke them individually and in response to individual delivery events.

What we will need to ensure is that they use the principle of Loosely Coupled systems that we learned in the 'Architectural Agility' chapter. This

---

57  I suspect that this is an area that AI and Machine Learning will be able to supplant people in the very near future.

mandates that the implementation specifics need to be *encapsulated* within the process definition. All calling processes, or notified processes, should be totally agnostic to any other processes' inner workings[58].

The first step in the design process, is to catalogue the known universe of processes. A lot of these should already exist, but some may be informal or not defined anywhere. Any gaps in existing process definitions need to be identified. These must be allocated to functional areas within the organisation, who will be responsible for their definition and ongoing maintenance. And of course, this demands an understanding and commitment to the endeavour from the relevant functional areas. Hopefully this won't be too difficult!

The Data Architect needs to consider how to bring the organisation on the journey to provide joined-up, holistic 'Data Governance Micro-services'. This will need a great deal of stakeholder engagement to implement. But, if well done, the transformation to the organisation will be spectacular!

Figure 89 may help you start to develop your own universe of processes.

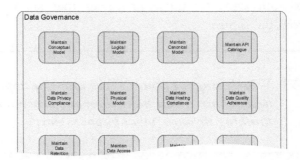

**Figure 89 – Define the universe of Data Governance processes**

A good source to start defining this universe, should be the Enterprise Toolkit patterns. This is because, each of these *must* have dedicated governance processes wrapped around it.

## Centre of the Universe Approach

The centre of the universe approach, provides a methodical way of working through all of the process definitions.

---

58    In fact, there is a clear parallel with Micro-services in our approach here.

The way it works is like this; concentrate on each process in turn and consider it as the 'centre of the universe'. Then determine which other processes it should *directly* trigger. Record each of these and define under what conditions the triggering would take place. Carefully agree with the appropriate stakeholders what (minimum) information needs to be supplied to the process to support its internal activities.

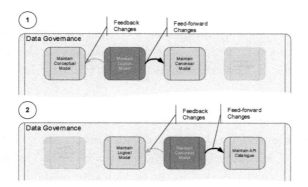

**Figure 90 – Make each process the centre of the universe in turn**

Remember to only consider those processes that are one degree of separation, from the centre.

---

*Principle 153*     ***When using the centre of the universe approach, never chain across more than one process, when thinking through 'what happens next'.***

---

## Start with the Enterprise Data Models

It makes sense to start with the Enterprise Data Models because:

- they are the cornerstone of the Data Governance framework

- we know how they interrelate already, and so mapping their triggered processes is easy

- they will start the 'ball rolling', allowing us to learn *how* to create the definitions, for less well known areas

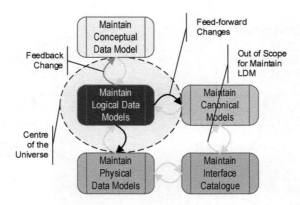

**Figure 91 – Start with the Logical Data Models**[59]

As we can see by comparing figure 91 with figure 29, this is easily accomplished, because we already know the way that the Enterprise Data Models are interrelated.

# Workflow Integration

We must reduce waste in processes. Thus a key area to focus on, is wherever we have baton handovers.

By aligning or integrating workflows, we can minimise waste by engaging the correct people, at the correct time, with the correct information. Ideally, this baton handover can be effected using a single workflow engine.

> *Principle 154*    **Linking the stakeholders, their processes and artefacts, through unified workflows, reduces 'idle time' and increases the overall efficiency of activities.**

This will have a dramatic impact on the overall processes, by reducing latency in both the Data Governance and delivery processes.

---

59   Compare this model with figure 29 on page 71.

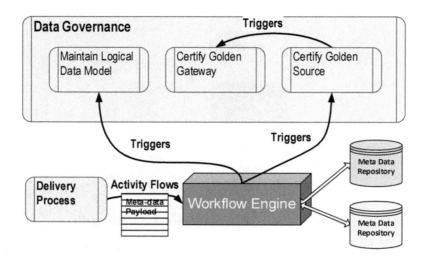

**Figure 92 – Unified workflow engine**

Figure 92 illustrates how the delivery processes can be integrated with Data Governance workflows, using a single unified workflow engine.

We also see that the Certify Golden Source process, triggers the Certify Golden Gateway process. But, notice that this is not triggered via the same workflow engine. As a result, this part of the chain of processes may not be *visible*. Potentially, this lack of visibility could prevent important metrics being captured that would otherwise allow us to optimise the overall process map.

## Auditors

In my experience, Auditors often ask questions that result in a lot of manual effort to provide answers for. Some questions might require several weeks of co-ordinated effort from those who already have day jobs!

To remedy this, a portal and reporting capability can be provided. This could even be possibly accessed directly by Auditors, who, where required, are able to drill-down to lower-level detail.

Making this a self-service process, will have a dramatic effect on reducing manual (wasted) effort.

# Dashboards

In the 'Agile Data Assurance' chapter, it was suggested that a key part of the overall process design, should be to capture metrics of the Data Governance processes. These metrics will allow bottlenecks to be identified and supports a constant focus on streamlining processes.

We can now see how the graphs on pages 102 and 103, can be achieved. In my opinion, a dashboard using metrics captured from the unified workflow repository, should be considered a core part of the Data Governance Framework.

---

**Principle 155** **A mandatory part of the Data Governance Framework should be the provision of a dashboard to report upon the efficiency of its processes.**

---

# Differentiated Workflows

The workflow payload design, should specify the *minimum* amount of information required to support the *appropriate* Data Governance processes. What comprises this minimum set, should be defined as a part of the integration of the Data Governance processes with those of delivery.

---

**Principle 156** **To reduce waste caused by inappropriate effort, workflows and their payloads should be tuned to their purpose, and only the appropriate Data Governance processes should be triggered.**

---

# Triggering the Data Governance Processes

Many, or (hopefully) all, of the Data Governance processes will already be in place. However, to make them integrate more easily with delivery, these may need to be re-engineered to be more atomic.

But this is not the biggest piece of work for us.

We have already established that the two sets of processes need to be decoupled, but how do we set about designing the way they are *invoked* from delivery?

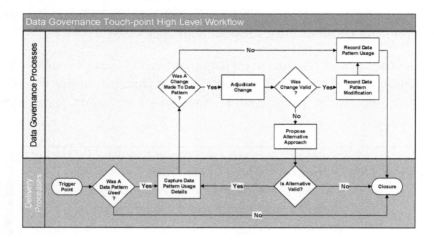

**Figure 93 – Triggering Data Governance processes from development**

Figure 93 provides a simple generic process model. The lower swim-lane, represents the delivery *triggering* actor, and the upper swim-lane represents a *triggered* Data Governance process.

This model can be used as the basis of the more specific models that define the integration of the two sets of processes.

The triggers need to be invoked when there are changes with a data impact, but from the delivery perspective. So as examples:

- Application for Master Data Domain consumption

- Extensions to a Logical Data Model

- Application to ratify new or modified Golden Source specifications

- Application to ratify new or modified Golden Gateway specifications

A useful quality assurance cross-reference for these, would be to use the Agents for Change catalogued as per figure 42, on page 107. Examine each of one of these, and analyse whether your trigger points will accommodate it.

## Delivery Work-stream Integration

How will we get the stakeholders embedded within the delivery work-streams to invoke the triggers that we have defined? We need to integrate these triggers with their practices, management and delivery tools. This might take the form of specialist User Story types that are integrated with the Sprint delivery User Stories. Perhaps as blocking sub-tasks, for example.

Wherever possible, there should be automatic triggering from the normal Development and delivery activities. This is especially important and actually very easily achieved using the Continuous Delivery software chain.

## Virtual Co-location

A major benefit from using an integrated workflow, is that the various stakeholders are able to access a unified source that can provide a transparent collective view. The feedback data flows from this can be used to streamline the related activities.

> *Principle 157* **A unified workflow engine can create virtual co-location, and provide shared access to all stakeholders that reduces the effort to monitor and verify the processes.**

It is also important to note that a further benefit of such a unified tool, is that it creates a sense of shared ownership and commitment to the overall processes.

## Missing Patterns – Driving Change

At the beginning of this chapter, we saw that there is a potential clash between the Data Governance processes that *manage* our data landscape, and the delivery processes that *modify* the system landscape.

We have looked at integration touch-points and the process definitions, but we have not yet made clear exactly how the processes will mesh. This must be implemented in a way that will enhance the outcome from each other's activities.

But we still have a problem to solve.

If we mandate the use of the Enterprise Toolkit's patterns, we need to ensure that it will always contain a required pattern at the time when delivery processes require it. But this seems to be a bit like magic. How will we predict what the Software Engineers will require ahead of time? In other words, how will we adapt the Toolkit to be ready for our needs next year, or even in five years from now?

The trick here is to detect and ratify changes to existing patterns, or create new patterns *before* they are required.

## Lag to Lead Processes

To complete in time, we know that the Data Governance processes cannot be triggered by the Software Engineers *during* the delivery activities. They will simply not be able to complete in time.

So how can the Data Governance processes make any necessary changes to the Enterprise Toolkit patterns with sufficient lead time, to complete ahead of a new delivery pattern requirement?

To solve this puzzle, we have to turn the Data Governance processes from *Lag* processes (e.g. the Gate Reviews) into *Lead* processes. These Lead processes will need to be triggered by specialist folk by them spotting 'bumps' on the delivery road ahead. It is they who will scan at least 4-6 weeks ahead, looking for novel requirements that the team will not be able to deliver using existing patterns.

### *The Eagle Team*

Typically, we should not leave this activity to the Software Engineers, but rather to those with Data Architectural abilities. They need to be able to assess the development impact of potentially sketchy 'requirements', and be sensitive to aspects of novelty.

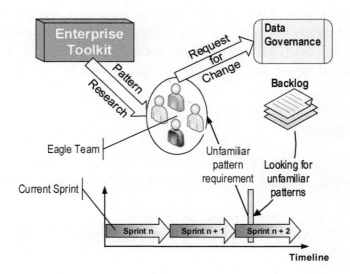

**Figure 94 – The Eagle Team triggering Data Governance processes**

Personally, I like the description 'Eagle Team', as it conjures up an image of an Eagle hovering above the landscape, scanning intently for the slightest pattern anomalies.

But whatever tag you give it, it will need to typically comprise members such as: Data Architects, Solution Architects or BAs.

This approach will shift the Lag processes normally encountered in delivery, to Lead processes.

There are two aspects to the requirement bumps on the road ahead, they represent a deficiency of:

1.  Patterns – e.g. no appropriate API signature

2.  Expertise – e.g. adoption of new Big Data Lake analytics

Let's look at these in more detail in the next sections.

## *Pattern Deficiency*

When Eagle Teams detect a potential bump on the road ahead, their next step should be to research the Enterprise Toolkit, looking for existing patterns that could satisfy all, or part, of the requirements.

However, it may be that there are no existing patterns available to satisfy a particular need. For example, no existing API has the required data attribution for the forthcoming requirements. This deficiency is resolved by providing feed-forward triggering of the appropriate Data Governance processes.

### Skills Deficiency

Even if the patterns do exist within the Enterprise Toolkit, there is a possibility that the delivery team don't have sufficient skills in these novel areas.

In these circumstances, further help may be requested from beyond the work-stream, including from:

- other development teams

- wider within the organisation

- external sources such as consultancies

## Methodology-Agnostic Integration

Irrespective of the methodology, there is consensus of the basics of the required activities for delivery. The common features of these activities, are illustrated in figure 95.

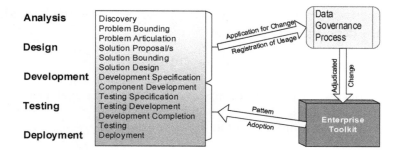

**Figure 95 – Generalised development activities**

Both SDLC and Agile have similar activities as indicated on this schematic.

It also illustrates that the highest probability of pattern deficiencies will be discovered during the predominantly Analysis and Design activities. Hence these activities will be the most likely to trigger the feed-forward Data Governance processes that modify the Toolkit patterns. During the delivery phases, we will simply be adopting pre-defined patterns and delivering these into the system landscape.

Let's see how this will work in practice.

We'll use common terms that have become prevalent with the shift to Agile DevOps methodologies. But actually these same trigger-points can equally be recognised within SDLC or other less formal approaches.

## Definition of Ready

Those activities that are to do with Analysis and Design, will use existing Enterprise Toolkit patterns within the specification of what is required from the subsequent delivery activities. This might be to identify and nominate the use of a Golden Gateway API, for example.

Where no patterns that fit the requirements exist, applications for change need to be made. This of course, is achieved by triggering the appropriate feed-forward 'change' Data Governance processes. By the time that the Software Engineers require the pattern, the processes will have had time to complete, and the pattern will be available for them to use. As a result the newly ratified Toolkit Pattern can be used as the basis for the Definition of Ready..

## Definition of Done

The delivery activities should have the specification for the delivery activities specified by an *existing* Toolkit Pattern. This could mean, for example, specifying the appropriate API required to consume the Customer headline attribution.

In other words the appropriate patterns should have already been made available to the Software Engineer at the time they are required.

All they have to do is record the use of the pattern in their delivery. With automated check-in or deployment techniques, this can be easily be integrated into the standard way of working. Obviously, this will increase its chances of being adopted!

## The Cycle of Success!

Figure 96 illustrates visually the previous descriptions for the way that we can integrate Data Governance processes with delivery processes, and at the same time boost the benefits to each.

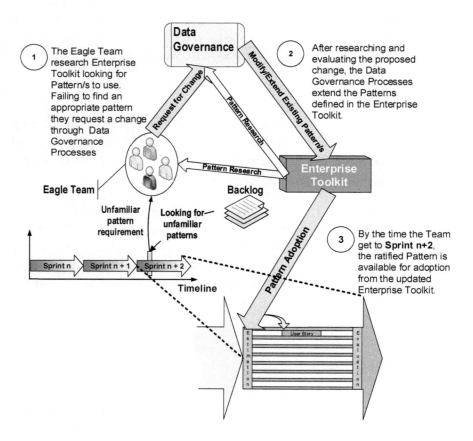

**Figure 96 – The Happy Path!**

But of course there will still be cases where the time taken for the governance processes, far outstrip the Eagle Teams forward-looking research. To cope with this we need to factor in Waiver processes as described in the next section.

## Waivers

If a Software Engineer needs to use an API that has not yet been accredited as a Golden Gateway, then should this be allowed?

There is a question of judgement here. If the requirement is 'urgent'[60] and it is generally accepted by the relevant stakeholders that the API *will* be certified, then we should prevent creating blocking dependencies. To do this, the uncertified API should be allocated a Waiver for its use. Obviously, all being well, the API will achieve the required certification, and the Waiver will no longer be required.

But note that this implies a periodic review of Waivers needs to be undertaken and built into its process. Of course, using the example above, these may determine that the API did not achieve accreditation. Therefore, processes will need to be defined for this eventuality as well as the successful outcomes.

---

60   If we are honest, it always seems to be urgent! But don't forget that there is the possibility of pushing the User Story back into the Backlog – at least this may buy some time.

# 9: Big Data

*We are entering a profoundly different world, where Big Data will redefine the human condition.*

Big Data is on the verge of changing our lives in profound and far-reaching ways as yet unimaginable. Individuals and organisations will have to rethink the way that they operate in this new world. The challenges are going to be enormous.

As ever, the thing that will remain constant for organisations, is the need to have a Data Architectural function that can safeguard and enhance their data usage. It will be of increased importance, throughout and beyond this period of seismic and uncertain change.

The characteristics heralding this new era, are obviously the vast data volumes and the new approaches that harvest and extract meaning from them. But what is interesting, is that many organisations and commentators are realising that it is the *meaning* derived from Big Data that is really what it's all about.

For many established organisations, Big Data needs to have context that is often revealed by combining it with the organisation's existing Master Data domains. This has resulted in a newly focussed awareness of the importance of controlling the meaning definitions of an organisation's data.

The Big Three Big Data themes that constantly grab headlines, are to do with social media, data privacy and commercial use of our personal data. But Big Data's impact is actually more fundamental, and all-embracing than suggested by concentrating on only these themes.

For Data Architecture too, there are some new ways of thinking required. These are as a result of the shift in the scope of data used within organisations. Embracing Big Data will result in changes to the Enterprise Data Models, and any corresponding Data Governance and MDM processes.

In this chapter, we will explore the basic features of Big Data to understand the changes it will cause to all of our futures. We will also examine some principles and models that will help guide us through this newly discovered, and rapidly evolving region of the Data Architecture landscape.

## What is Big Data?

It seems as if media and industry pundits cannot find enough to say about Big Data at the moment. However, the Big Data revolution has actually been creeping up on us for some time. In fact, arguably the initial shock waves are already over, and we are now in the phase of the aftershocks.

So what exactly does Big Data refer to?

Big Data is the all-encompassing name for harvesting and applying techniques to extract meaning from huge volumes of transactional data.

Obvious examples of the application of Big Data techniques include

- meteorological systems

- mobile phone location analysis

- gaming and betting behavioural analysis

In some ways, the examples above look quite different. But in fact, the underlying reliance on establishing patterns is a common characteristic of all of them.

Also, it should be understood, that it is the combination of Big Data's transactional patterns with the more humble structured data, where the real power of Big Data can deliver transformational outcomes. It is this structured data with which Data Architects are extremely familiar.

> *Principle 158* **For most established organisations, the full benefits of Big Data analysis are delivered when Big Data transactions are correlated to the meaning of its structured data, yielding unprecedented understanding of the Real World.**

For example, monitoring meteorological data is of interest in itself, but it is only when this is combined with other data, such as geospatial information that its true benefit to people is delivered. Providing analysis results such as the predicted path of a tornado, or projected rainfall patterns for farmers, for instance, can deliver dramatically positive outcomes. As the climate of our planet changes, these themes will become increasingly important.

In order to understand the impact of Big Data on organisations, let's look at a simple example.

A long time ago I renovated a derelict pub called The Turks Head in Wapping, London and converted it to a café that I crazily decided to run. Anyone who has knowledge of the catering industry, knows that one of its greatest challenges is having appropriate stock levels. Too much stock translates into lost profit, as perishable foodstuffs have to be thrown away. Too little stock results in lost opportunity sales and reputational loss; people rarely forgive a café that is unable to provide them with a coffee when they have made a trip specifically for this purpose!

Of course, knowing this ahead of time, I wrote a simple stock management system that recorded all of the purchases from suppliers, for each item in the café. Basic trend analysis was then applied to the recorded figures, allowing the average consumption rate of products to be ascertained. These raw consumption trends could then be modified by applying other factors such as the:

1.  averaged growth rate for the cafe overall

2.  figures from the same day in the previous week and

3.  figures from the same day in the previous year and

4.  ...

To begin with, I naively assumed that the results of such analysis would allow me to optimise the ordering of stock for the café. Almost immediately though, I realised that it was almost impossible to predict the number of customers for the following day to even ±50%!

Simple trend analysis was therefore of little practical benefit.

It struck me though, that there definitely *were* patterns to customer behaviours. Although, despite my best efforts, I could not make sense of any of them. Some simple factors were easy to spot. Mothers of toddlers were a large segment of the mid-week customer base. To my dismay, almost all of those that regularly attended the café, disappeared during the school summer holidays.

Other trends completely baffled me. I distinctly remember one Tuesday when it had been raining all day, the café was heaving with customers. Obviously with cafés, a big factor is that the fuller it is, the more attractive it becomes to passing footfall. This must have been a factor certainly. But on this particular Tuesday, we had several large, and uncharacteristic, reservations from people who could not possibly have known about the current levels of customers in the café. This is because they made the reservations from their workplaces several kilometres away. The following Tuesday we had very similar weather conditions, and yet the café experienced an absolute *dearth* of customers!

After discounting: the weather, the weather on the preceding day, the football results of the previous evening, the economic headlines, the 'people are already in there so it must be OK' factors, or anything else I could think of, I was left to conclude that there were *swarm* behaviours caused by complex factors, but that these were beyond my comprehension.

This simple example illustrates the drivers for organisations to make use of Big Data. They hope that analysis from it will provide insight into otherwise difficult to predict external factors that directly affect them.

It is this desire that has driven Big Data's ascendancy.

> *Principle 159  Big Data offers the seemingly impossible possibility, of being able to foretell future events with a high degree of certainty.*

If we return to the café example for a moment, ignoring privacy constraints and assuming that we could have been able to get access to peoples text messages, we may have been able to spot the use of terms indicating intentions to visit the Turks Head.

This would still not have been easy. It is highly unlikely that people would have texted each other with nice easy to analyse predictable strings like 'c u @ The Turks Head café, Wapping, London in 10 ☺'.

How would we know that a text that said 'usual place at 12.30?' was actually to do with a potential rendezvous at the café? This illustrates a problem that the structured world of data is ill-equipped to address. But, we'll see later how Big Data can unlock just this kind of analysis.

In the opening sections of this book, we introduced the concepts of *Known* and *Shareable*. These challenges to potential data usage, are at the very heart of Big Data. Let's see how in recent times these challenges have been increasingly overcome.

## Big Data's Big Bang

Of course, we have been predicting the future with small data trend analysis, and to a limited degree, with some Big Data for a long time. However, what we have witnessed in the last few years, is a *total transformation* of just what data *can* be analysed.

This has come about as a result of the step changes in the following

1. **Technological changes**

    a. Big Data management systems

    b. Processing power

    c. Storage capability

    d. Analysis tools

2. **Data harvesting mechanisms**

    a. Personal mobile devices

    b. Ubiquitous, cheap transponders

    c. Internet of Things

    d. Global telecommunications network

3. **Analytical advances**

    a. Innovative approaches to analysis

    b. Machine Learning

    c. Artificial Intelligence

4. **Commercial interest**

    a. Organisations feel the *need* to join the revolution to *survive*

    b. Explosive growth of Big Data services and products

5. **Social attitude changes**

    a. People feel the *need* to be part of the virtual global society (social networking)

    b. Lowering of personal privacy anxiety

These have, of course, been driven with complex inter-relationships, each helping knock over the barriers to changes in the others. But the combination of the preceding factors has reached a critical mass, whereby the impacts of Big Data are noticeably altering our lives.

Let's now look at some of the characteristics of Big Data in more detail.

# Harvesting Big Data

In the first chapter, we considered Control Systems that keep fighter aircraft in the sky and discovered that there are two types of data that impact aircraft flight. These are the:

1. Internal flight systems

2. External environment

Obviously, data from the flight systems is relatively easy to make use of, because it forms the systematised control systems' data flows. The other external data category would normally be captured through transponders that convert physical measurements into electrical signals. It is *far* more difficult to try to monitor *all* of the external environment data and obviously the idea of applying transponders everywhere on an aircraft is never going to fly[61]! This means that only limited external environmental data is available for aircraft.

Earlier though, we considered that the aircraft could be abstracted to a system and so can organisations. Both are inordinately complex, but both share the same characteristic of being able to monitor, record and understand the data that flows through their internal systems. In common with aircraft, what has previously been extremely difficult for organisations, was to make sense of the external environment that influenced its operations.

As a consequence, trying to use these externally driven influences to guide an organisation's strategies has, until recently, proved problematic.

For example, one of the most important factors for many organisations, is the consumer base of its products or services. Although understanding these has been of interest for many organisations for a long time, the problem for them has been to get useful, accurate, timely and statistically significant data.

Prior to Big Data, using techniques such as conducting surveys, or field trials, for example, was characterised by a number of analytical difficulties. These are partly due to the mechanisms used to collect the data. For example, the selection of a representative group and removal of skews caused by the collection mechanism itself, have always been major hurdles to overcome.

By contrast, people now constantly and unconsciously, record data through their devices connected to a global data network. This allows us to start analysing people's behaviours and opinions in previously inconceivable ways. Creating representative groups and removing mechanistic sampling skews is no longer the problem it was in the past.

## Known and Shareable

Although Big Data offers the seductive promise to reveal the future with as much certainty as the present, the *Known* and *Shareable* challenges remain. So let's examine how they relate to Big Data.

---

61   Sorry - couldn't resist it!

## Known Data - Big Data Farmers

We have witnessed the rapid growth in recent times of a whole new industry that is dedicated to harvesting and storing Big Data and providing Big Data analysis services.

These have radically transformed the *Known* data possibilities. Data about all sorts of Real World events and states is now readily available.

Predominantly, these fall into two categories, Big Data about:

1. the physical world

2. human activity

### Physical World

The obvious example of Big Data usage from the physical world is that of meteorological systems. Data concerning weather events has been recorded for hundreds of years. But recently, the proliferation of monitoring devices and phenomenal data processing power, has transformed our ability to analyse and predict weather patterns, with a high degree of accuracy, even at a micro-geospatial level.

In the last few years, there has been an explosion of cheap transponders and human willingness to install these. This has allowed a plethora of other diverse data, such as, seismological or air pollution levels to be recorded in real time and across geographically dispersed locations. Analysis from these is now redefining our understanding of the physical world. This will yield new possibilities such as earthquake predictions or warnings of severe pollution events.

And of course, we must not forget the relentless march of the Internet of Things. This new era is helping us to understand the usage patterns of products and components in far more detail - and often in near real-time.

Obvious advantages are to do with predicting failures, or maintenance requirements. But increasingly, we are also able to determine the human behaviour related to their usage.

### Human Activity

There is naturally a lot of interest in harvesting data related to human activity. This is being driven primarily by organisations that feel the need to understand the consumers of their products, in ways denied to them prior to the Big Data era.

As we are all very aware, people increasingly think nothing of leaking their opinions and intentions into the public domain using social media and internet forums. But there are many other aspects of human behaviour that are now being monitored and streamed.

One area in particular, is worthy of note and this is the realm of the human body. This relies upon devices that collect and often stream data about people's bodily functions. This may be combined with other reference data, such as their diet, location, age and gender.

This offers new ways of assessing physical well-being, and will almost certainly deliver a predictive capability that will allow us to shift healthcare from 'cure' to 'prevention'. Simple personal devices will compare the personal data profile with Big Data looking for patterns that indicate a future medical condition. If major conditions are detected early, they will be directed to health systems that are able to prescribe actions. This will exhibit a degree of predictive reliability that exceeds that of the current human-centric healthcare by orders of magnitude. And all of this can take place even before the individual would otherwise be aware that there is any looming problem!

### Shareable Big Data - Channel Selection

So, massive quantities of data of all descriptions is suddenly *Known*, but what does this mean for the *Shareable* set of data?

The explosion of *Known* data has not happened by accident, and is being driven primarily by commercial forces. As a result, there is now a large and rapidly growing number of commercial organisations, all very willing and able, to provide data and/or services that reveal answers to organisations' questions.

To an extent, this reduces the Big Data *Shareability* challenge to a matter of selecting the correct channel. Channel selection is all about being able to source the Big Data analysis that will yield reliable predictions, in the area of interest for an organisation.

## Big Data Companies as Mediators

A significant proportion of the organisations that harvest, store and provide Big Data, or the analysis from it, are taking on a mediator role between organisations that provide products and services, and their consumers. This newfound role is illustrated by figure 97.

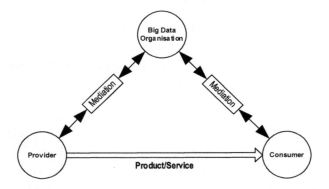

**Figure 97 – Big Data providers as mediators**

This schematic illustrates that the Big Data companies, not only provide analysis about Consumers to the Providers, but also analysis about the Providers to the Consumers.

It also shows the mediator niche that Big Data has created which is being rapidly filled by a new breed of Big Data organisations. These collectively form the backbone of the Big Data industry.

## Big Data Feedback Loops

If we return, for a moment, to the fighter aircraft analogy for organisations, and consider the problems they face flying at high speeds, and at very low altitude. In this flight condition they are extremely vulnerable to bumping into things! Power lines, or a hill, or even a tall tree, can present significant problems.

This risk is exacerbated because, by the time the pilot has noticed the obstacle it will be too late to carry out a manoeuvre to avoid it! To mitigate this, a specialised system reads the terrain ahead and if it detects a potential obstacle, it will immediately take avoidance action[62].

Many organisations feel that they too are hurtling forward at enormous velocity. They also feel extremely vulnerable to any changes on their horizon. For them, the potential obstacles in their path are represented in large degree, by the pace of technological and social behavioural changes. And for many, disruptive changes in their industry segment are also seen as potentially cataclysmic.

In addition, they feel unable to respond quickly enough to their unforeseeable future. This is partly because in many organisations, resilience and adaptability has been cut away long ago in attempts to reduce costs.

What these organisations crave, is a mechanism that is able to spot perturbations in the path of their trajectory. Ideally, this would provide them with sufficient warning to allow them to make a strategic manoeuvre that will avoid catastrophe. In addition, many organisations hope it will also provide them with a competitive advantage.

This exemplifies a problem that until recently, few organisations were able to solve. Before the advent of Big Data, the best that an organisation could hope for, was that a tsunami or drought of consumer activity would occur slowly enough to be detected by techniques like sales trend analysis. From these trend analysis predictions, it could hopefully take an appropriate course of action.

For predictive behaviour using external data, the approach relied on analysing a selected set of environmental factors thought to be causally linked to consumer trends. Analysis was carried out to determine the degree of probability that one was triggering the other. This is illustrated by the model in figure 98.

---

62    A bit like the Eagle Team in the previous chapter.

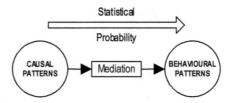

**Figure 98 – Causal prediction**

Causal analysis works well for simple components in a system. However, when components start to interact in complex ways, this simple form of analysis no longer yields high predictive reliability. This makes it of little use for complex systems and events in the Real World, such as weather patterns.

Of course, the realm of human behaviour often exhibits exactly this same complexity.

For example, if we think about trying to predict the price of shares in a listed company, we could take into account market factors for that company and evaluate whether the indicators we analyse, predict an upturn or downturn in the price.

This is illustrated in the graph in figure 99

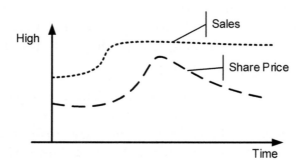

**Figure 99 – Share price boosted by sales figures?**

For the first part of the graph this works well, since the step change in sales drives up the price of the shares in a fairly predictable fashion. The problem with this approach is that actually share prices are not only controlled by factors directly linked to the company, such as sales, but also by human *sentiment.* This latter factor is complex, often irrational, and therefore, typically unpredictable.

Looking at the graphs again, although the sales remain high, the share price is driven relentlessly downward. Our simple causal trend analysis using sales alone, could not have predicted this.

However, if we could have analysed the purchasing sentiment for the shares, this would not only have predicted the initial rise in price, but would also have detected the sentiment shift that led to a downturn in the share price.

This is illustrated in figure 100.

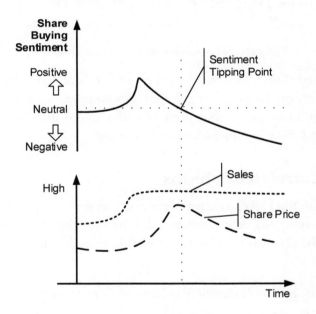

**Figure 100 – Share price versus purchasing sentiment**

By comparing the share price and purchasing sentiment, we see an immediate correlation.

The sentiment in our example, may still be causally driven, but by stimuli that we are unable to monitor directly. For example, a new entrant into the market, or launch of competitor product, or departure of a senior executive, may all lead to a negative sentiment.

We cannot feasibly monitor all the possible causal stimuli!

But why even try, if we can monitor the sentiment that results from the complex set of shifting swarm behavioural stimuli?

When considering complex human behaviour, we now have an analysis tool with a far higher degree of reliability, than previously possible. This is illustrated in figure 101.

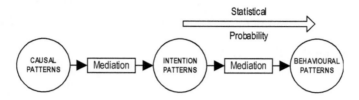

**Figure 101 – Analysing human sentiment**

Notice though, that although we are not reliant on identifying and monitoring *any* of the *causal* stimuli that *drive the intention patterns,* figure 101 illustrates the assumption that there is still a causal link between human sentiment and the subsequent human behaviours.

## Big Data Correlated Patterns

The advent of Big Data has utterly transformed the way we can understand the world by analysing data. Until now, for the vast majority of data analysis, we have only been able to establish simple causal links from stimuli to outcomes.

However, the sheer volumes of Big Data in so many new areas, provides a new way of understanding the world.

> *Principle 160* *The collection of Big Data, allows the application of analysis techniques that take us beyond the causal realm and into one of associative correlation.*

Although this field of analysis is not new in itself (think of medical research), what has changed, is the way that the technique can now be brought to bear on a wide range of types of readily available *Shareable* data. We are at an unprecedented point in human history, where we are able to collect large and seemingly disparate sets of data that may have a high degree of correlated association. And these are revealing previously un-imagined realms of understanding, and predictive insights.

To understand the lack of causal dependency let's take a very simple example. It might just be that the combination of the following factors has a high degree of association with the likelihood that a person will not suffer a stroke in later life -

- the supermarket chain they shop at

- their residential post code

- their choice of browser provider

- their predilection for rock music

However, there is *no causal link* being suggested here; even if there is a very high degree of correlated association, adopting these lifestyle choices will not mean you will necessarily join this fortunate group!

---

**Principle 161**  **Big Data provides the possibility that patterns in data can reveal a high degree of associative correlation with other patterns, without needing to establish any causal link between them.**

---

In addition, by combining different types of Big Data, we can reveal ever more possible types of insights.

This gives us a glimpse of the exciting possible future uses of Big Data, which will almost certainly enhance our understanding in ways we have not yet even dreamt of.

## Conforming Meaning

Principle 4 stated that for organisations, the universally understood and agreed *meaning* of data is everything.

This is as true for Big Data as for any other type of data.

---

**Principle 162  For Big Data, its universally understood and agreed meaning is everything.**

---

In earlier sections, we saw that meaning for structured data can be abstracted into domains. We need to consider how this concept translates into the realm of Big Data.

There are essentially two types of Big Data domain conformance:

1. simple meaning
2. complex meaning

## Simple Meaning – Single Domain Master Data

Historically, our approach for structured data within an organisation's scope, has been to remove the 'noise' surrounding simple transactions and construct a meaning framework for them. For certain types of Big Data analysis this approach is still applicable.

As an example, when considering simple measurement data that is internal or external to an organisation's systems, the *meaning* is relatively unambiguous.

If we imagine a chemical plant temperature sensor, it may be using a specific measurement scale, for instance, Celsius or Fahrenheit, but for this type of Big Data, the content and meaning of the message are easy to determine. Similarly, monitoring the electrical fingerprint of a fridge freezer to reveal problems, or predict faults, only requires the sampling of Voltage measurements over time.

## Complex Meaning – Analytic Conformance

How can we possibly join a Tweet to our Product Domain? This just does not seem feasible.

In this category of Big Data, it is not possible to conform the data directly to simple deterministic Domains. This is because the *meaning* of the data is often very hard to gauge from individual instances.

The approach adopted is to typically use sophisticated analysis techniques, for example:

- statistical analysis
- algorithmic techniques
- sentiment/lexical analysis[63]

These approaches are often described as yielding *insights* from the data.

---

**Principle 163**  **Big Data extends our ability to understand the world by looking for patterns that correlate to meaning, and abstracting these to reveal insights.**

---

This principle is illustrated in figure 102.

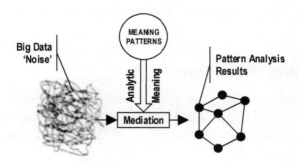

**Figure 102 – Applying meaning to Big Data**

Notice though, that this technique can be extended to conform the patterns of Big Data to the *meaning* enshrined in Master Data.

Although not easy to implement, this allows us to combine the purchasing

---

63    In the first chapter we saw the importance of linguistic sciences and techniques in order to establish *meaning* from data. These can have even more significance when analysing the meaning of Big Data.

sentiment for shares to specifically related stock, as in our earlier example.

Figure 103 shows this concept of using Big Data with an organisation's Master Data, to produce previously unachievable analysis.

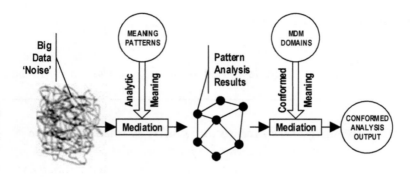

**Figure 103 – Joining Big Data to Master Data**

To make this happen in reality, means creating relationships between an organisation's Master Data and the meta-data that is used to drive the analysis.

## Data Meaning Transition

What the preceding sections indicate is a grey-scale spectrum for frameworks of *meaning*. This spectrum varies from the highly normalised, structured world of systematised data, to the messier world of Big Data transactions.

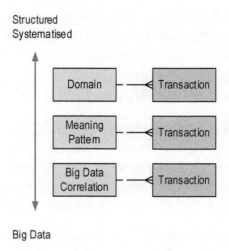

Structured
Systematised

Big Data

**Figure 104 – Data meaning transition**

Figure 104 illustrates the way that as we transition from the highly structured data world to the world of Big Data, we need to change the basis for creating its meaning framework.

# Big Data Adoption Impact

For many organisations, the adoption of Big Data will represent a paradigm shift in the way that they use data to benefit the organisation. This section provides the following areas to consider:

1. Data Governance Framework

   a. Framework process definitions

   b. Legal implications

   c. Enterprise Data Models

2. New dependencies

These are described below.

## Extending the Data Governance Framework

Typically, established organisations that start to embrace Big Data, will neither be harvesting, nor providing the analytical systems that provide them with the Big Data analysis outcomes. As a result of the adoption of Big Data they will almost certainly need to adapt its Data Governance Framework. These changes will be required to extend and modify definitions and processes, to allow them to control the new data usage.

## Data Governance Framework Processes

For some organisations, the way that the new processes need to be defined may be very different from their existing processes. This can arise where, for example, they require engagement with, and ongoing commitment from, an external organisation. The creation of such processes will therefore present new challenges, and these may not necessarily be trivial.

For example, if using *and becoming dependent* on data hosting, AI and Machine Learning capabilities from a Big Data organisation, what will happen if the organisation wants to, or *needs* to exit the arrangement?

Sharing the risk across several providers may make sense, but the exit strategy needs to be clearly defined. These factors need careful consideration, as the impact on the organisation can be dramatic if things go wrong.

## Legal Implications

In addition to the process definitions, the changes required to the Data Governance Framework, may mean that an organisation moves into totally unchartered legislative and regulatory territory. Some will need to ensure that they have the expertise and experience, to make these agreements successful.

For example, if an organisation starts to analyse data about people, it may need to ensure it remains compliant with prevailing Data Privacy legislation. This is an area of compliance that will continue to change rapidly. Organisations need to be aware of this, and accept that this may demand constant changes to their own use of the data, and also continual modifications to their system landscape.

As an example; what happens if they have become operationally reliant on a Big Data product that is unable to conform to new compliance requirements?

Another factor to consider as a result of Big Data adoption, is that the stakeholders involved in the Data Governance Framework, may require additional legal expertise and advice. Where these are not already present, adding legal expertise to the Data Governance processes becomes essential.

## Extending the Enterprise Data Models

In chapter 2 it was stated that accurate data models within an organisation's data scope, will remain true representations over extended periods of time.

But, we need to tackle a conundrum raised by many folk in the arena of Big Data adoption. They often assert that with the advent of Big Data, our data models are no longer useful, or even relevant and we should discard them.

Whilst I *strongly contest* this view, what is almost certain is that adopting Big Data will cause the Logical Data Models to be *extended* to support its new data realms.

A primary driver for organisations wanting to adopt Big Data, is the need to focus on external events and their data 'vapour trails'. This is so that the organisations can understand what is happening in their external operational environment.

The typical example given, is that the organisation will be able to 'understand its customers more fully'. This example is supported by the evidence of organisations increasingly communicating messages and offerings to their customers that are *highly attuned* to each customer's *specific profile*.

Organisations that have started to embrace this external environmental data, must revisit any Enterprise Data Models that were built prior to this era. These earlier data models are often characterised as being organisation-centric, operationally focussed and hence, introspective in their scope.

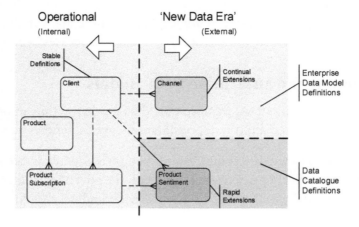

**Figure 105 – Extended data model scope**

Figure 105 illustrates a data model fragment to typify three areas for the Enterprise Data Models to consider:

1. Operational domains – existing

2. External domains – extensions

3. Analysis domains – highly volatile

Let's examine these in a little more detail in the following sections.

## Operational Domains

The Operational areas of our data models will remain largely unchanged (hopefully) - even in this new data era. This is because they reflect the structured data supporting the internal operations of the organisation and, as we saw earlier, they must be mechanism-agnostic. In other words, even if the *way* we carry out activities becomes re-engineered, the data models should not require corresponding revisions.

Note though that they may need to incorporate future-proofed and extensible structures, to support Localised or Extensible Attribution, as described earlier on page 58. However, we will not need to constantly revise the models, as concrete structures can be defined that provide this capability, without the need for us to constantly revamp their definitions, in response to change.

## *External Domains*

As many of us are aware, in the last few years many organisations have undergone a Digital Marketing revolution. This is a good example of the need for organisations to rethink the way that they interact with their operational environment in this data-rich era.

The resulting refocus will cause the data models that underpin the interactive operations of our organisations to be reviewed, and possibly extended. These extensions will be needed to reflect the new modes through which they can interact with their external worlds, e.g. Channels for Marketing, or for Product, or Service fulfilment.

But notice that these new realms still need to be related back to key Entities in the Operational area of the models. For example, if we think about Client Product Preferences, these *must* have Relationships back to the Client and Product Entities.

Although the data world is changing rapidly, the volatility of *these* new data domains, still takes place sufficiently slowly to justify the effort to define them in the Enterprise Data Models.

## *Analytical Domains*

The third area of the data models is where the white heat of change prevails, and the definitions within this scope will be highly volatile. As a result, they will almost certainly *never* be part of the Enterprise Data Models. Or, if they are, they are likely to be represented in generic, highly meta-data driven data structures. These may result in their meaning being obscured to all but Data Modellers and Data Scientist specialists.

When people assert that Logical Data Models are no longer relevant, it is often an opinion that is rooted in this area. As long as the opinion is *bounded to this region*, then I agree with it.

And yet, we *must still catalogue them*. This is so that their *meaning* can be shared by the consumers of the data analysis.

This raises the thorny question of *where* they will be catalogued.

This is definitely not an easy question to answer. You will have to find a way to disseminate the definitions of the data to the consumers, or prospective consumers. Possibly, for example, this could take the form of a dynamic catalogue made available within the reporting capability itself.

But of course, this would limit the sharing of these meanings to a very small set of stakeholders. Although this sounds worrying, it may be a perfectly acceptable constraint. This is because, the people who will be interested in the analysis, will be purely focussed from a strategic, marketing or Kaizen perspective. As a result, they will naturally only form a small part of the organisation's functions.

Again though, notice that for the vast majority of our organisations, these new insights are only relevant in the *context* of the data models' areas that we have already described in the preceding sections. This means that, at some level, they must still *integrate* with the preceding areas of the data models. For example, this typically determines that as a minimum, they must have relationships back into our Master Data Domains.

## New Dependencies

For most organisations starting to adopt Big Data to support their operations, there will be new dependencies that they will need to carefully consider.

We are moving into a world where some Big Data companies are able to orchestrate the whole product fulfilment chain from; influencing product selection, to enabling the purchase and even providing the product distribution, as indicated by figure 106.

**Figure 106 – Big Data organisations as intermediaries**

This new relationship offers tremendous opportunities for enterprises to start-up and rapidly grow, with few of the major hurdles that offered insurmountable barriers, even ten years ago. However, the flip side to this opportunity is that the *exposure* of the Products and Services to the consumers is increasingly *determined by* the Big Data companies.

Whilst this relationship is generally on an equitable basis today, can this be relied upon into the future?

## Datopia

Datopia is my description for the new era of human development where systematised and digitised data, is far more important to society than the Real World.

These days almost everywhere we go and everything we do, leaves little vapour trails of *Shareable* data. Much of this is to do with the devices that we use and of course, mobile phones are foremost amongst these. Also however, we are sharing our most intimate details with Big Data organisations in ways that signal a fundamental redefinition of our perception of being private individuals.

We are all aware of the trend, in the last decade, of devoting increasing time and effort to creating and maintaining our virtual selves. These virtual selves and the complex social networks that we have constructed around them, demand ever higher levels of maintenance by us. The resulting streams of data from this activity, are all being harvested, winnowed, stored and then sold on to the Big Data organisation's customers.

Currently, we are on the verge of these profound shifts in social behaviours and our relationships with Big Data companies, causing real shock waves in the human condition.

In the early 1900s, the Marxist philosopher Antonio Gramsci, described Cultural Hegemony and the mechanisms through which human social behaviour is controlled and propagated. The premise of this theory is the imposition of a dominant value system that determines the norms of societal interactions and received values. At the time, Gramsci applied this theory to the class struggle and ascribed the dominant value system to the ruling or upper classes. He characterised it as being a tool used by these classes to oppress and obtain acquiescence of the working class.

However, when we consider the impact of Big Data in determining what you will 'also like', search engines prioritising links and a myriad of other more subtle influences that 'customise' your experience, we realise that the impact of Big Data is certainly that of creating a new and potent hegemonic value system.

**We show all the signs of increasingly embracing this new hegemonic system to determine our attitudes and behaviour.**

Personal devices, telecommunication networks, the internet and Big Data, are all acting in concert to supplant many of the established hegemonic processes.

This is illustrated in the simple feedback loop in figure 107.

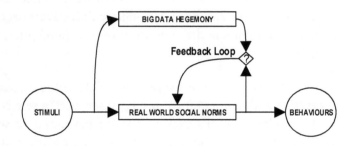

**Figure 107 – Big Data Hegemony**

We are also all aware of the rapid erosion of authoritative information sources. We can choose opinion over fact. As a result, swarm behaviour will replace objectivity.

These pivotal changes to value system propagation, will change our future lives in ways of which we are as yet unaware. But of concern is that the power we are handing to these organisations is unprecedented and driven largely by commercial and political pressures.

Will these shifts be beneficial to us overall?

## Big Data is Watching You

In George Orwell's famous book titled Nineteen Eighty-Four, he conjured up a future where the subject of the story, Winston, works for the

Department of Information rewriting history to fit the needs of the Party[64].

Big Brother watches over every aspect of peoples' lives, vigilantly looking for any signs of non-conformance with the regime.

The current world of personal data *Shareability* would have made the ruling elite in Orwell's dystopian vision very happy indeed. People now reveal the tiniest minutiae of their lives, and even their innermost thoughts, in ways unthinkable when this classic was written. Social networks and the interactions between individuals in these networks, are all being monitored and analysed.

Big Data will provide the necessary analysis fodder to feed AI and Machine Learning. These will be able to understand you, as an individual, infinitely better than anyone you know does – including you!

By understanding the human condition with ever more precision, our behaviours and what dictates them will become revealed. Once the drivers for why we do, what we do, are understood, brand-washing will leave us vulnerable to organisations triggering compulsive behaviours in us. Not only will we be defenceless against such manipulation, but we will probably even be totally unaware that we *are* being compelled and by what means.

In order to be a successful economic unit in this new world order, will we need to submit to the controllers of it? Will failure to comply mean exclusion?

This may affect all areas of human endeavour from employment and healthcare, to housing and education.

If this seems a little far-fetched, just consider who it is that 'owns' *your* credit rating? How would it affect your life if their algorithms made a mistake in assessing your rating that prevented your access to loans or credit cards for instance? Then imagine if your ability to remedy this involved significant

---

64    Interestingly, the judgement (Case C131/12 13 May 2014) in the EU court of Justice provides for individuals to seek the suppression from internet search engines' results, of web links relevant to them!
Thus, if, following a search made on the basis of a person's name, the list of results displays a link to a web page which contains information on the person in question, that data subject may approach the operator directly and, where the operator does not grant his request, bring the matter before the competent authorities in order to obtain, under certain conditions, the removal of that link from the list of results

effort or expense, or was reliant on legal action, or was just not possible!

In this vision of Datopia, the tables have been turned and instead of Big Data being our beneficial servant, it has become an indomitable tyrant.

# 10: Agile Data Flows

*Aligning our data flows, will liberate their organisational benefit and deliver surefooted agility.*

On our journey so far, we have learned a great deal about the essential concepts, principles and models that will allow us to maximise the benefit from our data.

The job of this chapter, is to describe the practical application of these building blocks, so that they can deliver dramatic transformations to our organisations.

In the Seven Principles of Data chapter, we described how data provides the essential lifeblood of our organisations. This description of it as the lifeblood, refers to the idea that its data flows are *essential* to deliver its operations and determine its strategic direction. Whilst always true in the past, this is becoming ever more critical. We are now on the verge of disruptive step changes in the *primacy* of data.

Let's examine this concept in a little more detail.

Increasingly all organisations are becoming data organisations. For many, their *entire essence* exists purely as data. Think of loans, or insurance products that most of us are subject to. They are not 'real' objects in any sense; they are wholly manifested through data definitions. In many cases, this data will rarely see the light of day outside of a system landscape.

> *Principle 164*  *For increasing numbers of organisations, all of their operations exist solely as data, even their products and services are not tangible objects at all - they are purely constructed from data.*

With the unstoppable advance of 'the machines', even many of those products that *are* physically tangible, are built by robots using automated assembly lines. This mechanical organism's nervous system, is controlled and coordinated by data patterns defined in one or more systems. The fabrication processes are monitored by a bewildering array of sensors. These constantly stream data into algorithms for analysis. The algorithms tirelessly analyse this data for patterns that reveal opportunities to optimise the processing.

They will *immediately* react to incoming data. For example, to fine-tune processes to reduce the cost of production, or even ramp up production due to *anticipated* demand.

Product design has been a last bastion of human creative input. But even this area is increasingly subject to analysis of consumption and feature use. This results in an understanding of how the products can be designed or enhanced to be ever more appealing. Even now the formulation of films or TV series is being tuned in response to feedback from audiences to previous content. A possibility going forward is that when we consume the same entertainment media as others, the content will be further tuned to our preferences. So even if we are listening to the same song, it will be adapted to our preferences, emphasising the brass backdrop, or raising the tempo, or even cutting out whole sections based upon our tastes.

In terms of product distribution, where this relies on physical delivery, even the delivery logistics are all simply data somewhere in a system landscape. Increasingly, even after delivery, algorithms analyse product usage to yield insights as to how they can be optimised to reduce maintenance, or predict failures.

The trends that we all witness, are accelerating a reliance on data for *all* aspects of the modern world. We are all aware of these seismic changes, but it is worth underlining them.

## Increasingly, very few humans will be significantly involved in any part of an organisation's product lifecycle.

## Data will *drive* their product processes, including: design, marketing, production, payment and fulfilment.

This understanding highlights the dependency of our organisations on *healthy data flows*. Without these, at best, our organisations will operate sub-optimally. At worst, the green shoots of the disruptors, will quickly grow to overtake them, and they will simply wither and die.

---

**Principle 165** *Healthy agile organisations are ever more reliant on healthy agile data flows.*

---

At the same time, the proportion of custom systems that organisations develop has plummeted. Instead of bespoke system development, these days, they increasingly adopt 'Everything as a Service'. Often their backbone systems are hosted *somewhere* in the Cloud. The internal architectures and data structures of these are unknown, often unknowable, and simply not relevant for the organisation to care about.

As a consequence, the historic emphasis on bringing Data at Rest definitions under control, is of marginalised importance.

---

**Principle 166** *We are becoming far more concerned with understanding Data at Flow, than Data at Rest, and we must ensure it conforms to our agreed definitions of its meaning.*

---

However, development does still take place. Predominantly, this is in the construction of aggregation hubs.

These points of confluence of our data, provide the 'big picture' of our data estate. From them, we can report on this estate, and make it available to downstream consumers. Typically, this capability involves: Operational Data Stores, or Data Warehouses (still!), or Big Data Lakes.

In this chapter, we'll discover how we can *maximise the benefits* of bringing the data together, whilst *minimising the effort* to do so.

# We're All (Becoming) Data Integrators Now

Not many organisations would dream of creating a Customer Relationship Management (CRM) system from scratch these days. Yet in the past, I have helped develop many of these from the ground up. This exemplifies the current trend away from custom development. Increasingly, organisations are using COTS products and basing their data systems 'in the Cloud'.

Although the rationale for these decisions is compelling, we shouldn't ignore that the fact that implementing these capabilities is not always easy.

But, however we look at it, it simply no longer makes sense for us to custom build a whole host of our core operational systems.

As a result of the above trends, our organisations will increasingly need to act as data integrators. A key pre-requisite in this era, is for us to adopt a Loosely Coupled approach to our system landscapes. This will provide us with the agility our organisations crave. However, in turn it predicates that the interfaces conform to our Enterprise definitions.

> *Principle 167  Those organisations that can deliver systems into a well-defined Loosely Coupled landscape, will almost certainly succeed into the future, those that don't will increasingly struggle.*

This shift in emphasis is always brought into sharp relief where the data is being transported from disparate sources into a consolidation capability. For any ill-prepared organisation, this can be an extremely painful undertaking.

Let's see how we can avoid this pain, and liberate true organisational agility through some very simple data management techniques.

# Consolidation Hubs

Consolidation Hubs draw data from a range of Mastering Systems and persist it in a centralised capability. Some of these sources, for example, will be:

- legacy systems
- COTS products implemented in the Cloud

- third party data provided through APIs

Yet, whatever their flavour, the purpose of the hub is to bring these disparate sources together. It is designed to provide a 'centralised'[65] source of common understanding for subsequent interrogation and distribution. Although I never hear mention of it, this common understanding demands that the Enterprise Data Models *must* be used.

If they are, they will deliver massive benefits.

> **Principle 168  Successful Consolidation Hubs will have used the Enterprise Data Models to assure the common understanding of their data.**

Earlier, in figure 58, we saw an example of a specialised Consolidation Hub for Master Data. In this chapter, we will look at the principles that can be applied, irrespective of the nature of the data. Figure 108 illustrates a common pattern, where data is consumed into a centralised repository.

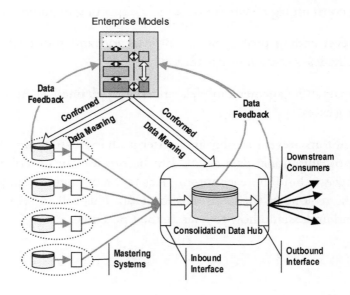

**Figure 108 – Generalised Consolidation Hub**

---

65    Of course this centralised capability may be virtually centralised but actually dispersed geographically due to performance or Data Hosting constraints for example.

Sometimes the organisation characterises this hub as a Reporting Platform, sometimes it will be a Big Data Lake. But, however it is badged, let's see how we can begin to bring a degree of control over the data flows both, into it, and out of it.

# Data Flows And Consolidation Hubs

Without the adoption of a few simple techniques to bring conformance to our data, a Consolidation Hub can fail to yield any significant benefit. Even worse, it can sometimes become a significant drain on an organisation's resources and its consumers' patience!

These errant hubs often exhibit the following characteristics:

- Inability to provide a catalogued and understood description of its data

- Difficult and lengthy lead times for data ingestion

- Ever increasing maintenance and customisation costs

- A constant lag to satisfy consumers' reporting requirements

- Never-ending prototyping, tool selection and proof of concept activities – consumer frustration

- Opaque engagement models and poorly defined SLAs and BAU processes

These symptoms reveal strong anti-patterns that frustrate any hope of delivering organisational data agility. But before we can describe how to treat the *causes* behind these symptoms, let's take a moment to simplify, and describe the regions of the Consolidation Hub. This will allow us to focus on each and understand how to liberate their potential.

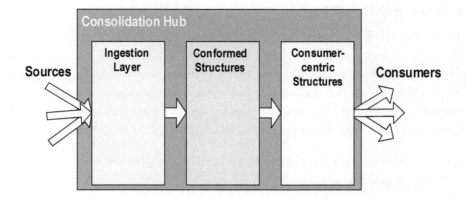

**Figure 109 – The three simplified regions of a Consolidation Hub**

Figure 109 illustrates the three typical transformation layers:

1. Ingestion Layer

2. Conformed Structures

3. Consumer-centric Structures

We'll examine what is required from each of these layers, in the following sections.

## Ingestion Layer

As its name implies, the Ingestion Layer is where the data is delivered into our Consolidation Hub's scope.

Often, the construction of Operational Data Stores, or Data Warehouses, has been relatively measured. Typically, they have been designed and developed after thorough analysis of their source data. As a result, clearly documented understanding of the data *prior* to its ingestion has been agreed. This is mainly because their 'rigid' internal data structures could not have been built without understanding the profile of the source data.

However, even for them, this has not always been true. And it is becoming ever more difficult to do this. Imagine the Loosely Coupled landscape. We do not know, and quite possibly can never know, the internal data structures of the various Cloud hosted COTS products whose data is being ingested.

# Big Data Swamps

More worrying has been a consequence of the headlong rush to ingest data into hastily constructed Big Data Lakes. In many organisations, this focussed on the 'ingestion' of as many sources as possible and as quickly as possible. Often this has resulted in some basic principles being dropped on the floor. One of the most important of these principles, is the need to demand a 'manifest' describing exactly what data is being ingested.

This detailed declaration should have been demanded *before* any source of data was ingested.

For hubs that ignored this basic pre-condition, although the delivery of data *into* them has been rapid, extracting any useful benefit *from* them, has often been far less successful.

---

**Principle 169**  *As a result of not cataloguing ingested data definitions, many Big Data Lakes have rapidly descended into becoming muddy Data Dumps.*

---

There are many complex and interrelated reasons why this is the case, but we can take some basic precautions that will dramatically reduce the problem.

# Tightly Coupled – Agility Anti-Pattern

Although we often do not 'know' the contents of our Big Data Lakes, given enough time and resource, we can eventually catalogue them. But, there is a second significant problem that is rarely mentioned. Initially this may not even be noticed, however, in the longer term it can be actually be far more debilitating.

This occurs as a result of the data being delivered 'verbatim' to the Ingestion Layer. This harks back to the era of Point to Point data flows and is obviously an agility anti-pattern.

Let's look at a real life example of this.

An in-house CRM was being replaced by a COTS Cloud based solution. The replacement roll out programme was planned to take several years across the globe. But the original system's data had been ingested verbatim into a Big Data Lake for reporting purposes. This approach raised two significant hurdles to the ingestion of the replacement system's data:

1. New ingestion processes and onward flows for the new system's data became additional work for the Consolidation Hub team

2. As each Country was migrated from the old source to the new, consistent and holistic global reporting still needed to be provided *across the two systems*

Naturally, to make this source's transition successful, required a great deal of effort from the *Consolidation Hub's team*. This resulted in unnecessary costs, delays, frustration and poor data quality.

> **Principle 170** *If a Consolidation Hub is Tightly Coupled to its sources, any internal changes to these, or wholesale replacements, will require a spike of activity by the Consolidation Hub team.*

Eventually the Consolidation Hub team can become submerged in an unachievable backlog of change requirements from all of its Source Systems. Quite obviously therefore, we should see this Tightly Coupled approach as a strong anti-pattern.

> **Principle 171** *Ingesting source data verbatim into a Consolidation Hub is an absolute anti-pattern.*

Instead, we must ensure that our approach is based upon the principles we learned about in the 'Architectural Agility' chapter.

## Whose IP Is It Anyway?

For many Consolidation Hubs, the principle of encapsulating the IP of the data in the source system has been ignored.

It is self-evident that the team best placed to make sense of the source data, and conform it to the Enterprise definitions, is the source delivery team. The least well qualified to do this work, is the Consolidation Hub delivery team. Too often this basic tenet is forgotten.

Figure 110 illustrates how the principle of encapsulating the source IP[66] applies to the Consolidation Hub flows, illustrated in figure 108.

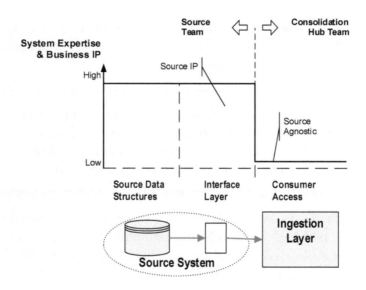

**Figure 110 – Encapsulating IP in the source systems [67]**

Hopefully, in your organisation, the source team will have already done the work to define *ratified* interfaces. Of course, these need to be aligned to the Enterprise Data Models.

If this can be achieved, then it provides an approach to simplify ingestion and provide true agility from our Consolidation Hubs. This is described in the next section.

---

66   As described on page 168.
67   Note that in the graphical part of figure 110, the Ingestion Layer of the Consolidation Hub is viewed as the consumer of the Mastering System.

# The Green Channel

We are all aware of the idea of Green Channels to speed flows of passenger ingestion at airports. This relies on the idea that the individuals (effectively) self-declare conformance with the entry criteria.

We can adopt an analogous approach for our data. The entry criteria for our data, is obviously conformance with the Enterprise definitions and structures.

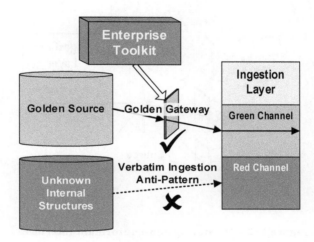

**Figure 111 – Accelerated data ingestion via the Green Channel**

Therefore, *before* ingesting data from any source, we would be wise to demand that the consumption *must* be via a ratified interface.

> **Principle 172  Data from source systems must only be ingested using ratified interface specifications conformed to the Enterprise Models.**

But of course, not every source will have adopted this conformed interface definition approach. In these circumstances, as a condition of the ingestion of its data, the source must undertake the construction of a conformed interface to be used for the ingestion.

Also, we need to consider data consumed from externally provided interfaces. We cannot demand that these sources conform their interfaces to our definitions. Their interfaces are provided to many other consumers. Consider as an example, the requirement to ingest Credit Rating Agency data from a variety of providers. Each will have their own APIs defined using their own definitions. A simple trick here is to abstract these definitions and create and maintain an internally defined organisation-centric interface.

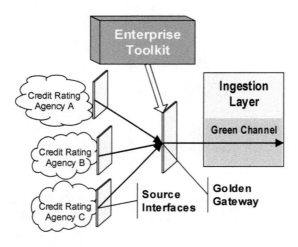

**Figure 112 – Re-stating non-conformant interfaces**

The internally defined Golden Gateway will re-state the externally provided data, using definitions that are conformed to the Enterprise Data Models.

## De-coupling Consolidation Teams

If we can successfully implement the Green Channel approach, we can fast-track all Logical Data Model compliant data ingestion. This will allow the Consolidation Hub folk to concentrate on providing sophisticated data capabilities for their consumers in an agile manner.

> *Principle 173  The Barrier to Entry can be reduced to insignificance, by only allowing ingestion from source systems through ratified interface definitions.*

The advantages to this approach are numerous and include all of the advantages described earlier in the 'Architectural Agility' chapter. However, let's look at the commonly encountered problem we described earlier, where an organisation was transitioning from a custom CRM to a COTS Cloud-based replacement.

If our Green Channel approach had been originally adopted, then the transition from one system to the other, would have been seamless as illustrated in figure 113.

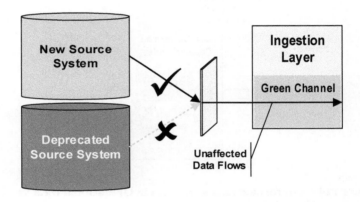

**Figure 113 – Source system-agnostic Green Channel ingestion**

Of course, as a consequence all the consumers of the data from the Ingestion layer on, would have been unaware of the transition from one source to the other. As a result, the reporting based upon the two systems data would be unaffected by the new system adoption. Naturally, the Consolidation Hub team were aware of the transition, but needed to do very little to accommodate the change.

What this clearly highlights, is that as more sources are plugged in through the Green Channel ingestion, we are able to flow their data up to the Conformance Layer with negligible effort.

## Conformance Layer

For the Conformed Data Structures there will also be variations for each of the Consolidation Hub styles. Let's look at these in a bit more detail.

## Operational Data Stores

For Operational Data Stores, the basis of the Conformed Data Structures should be the Enterprise Physical Data Models. These in turn should show little variation from their related Logical Data Models.

This approach is illustrated in figure 114.

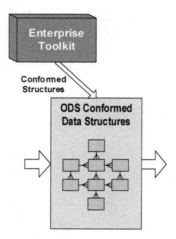

**Figure 114 – Conformed data structures in Operational Data Stores**

However, most consumers of Operational Data Stores' data want it to be presented in an easily accessible set of data structures, and we'll see how to provide this later in this chapter.

## Data Warehouses

Data Warehouses will typically have used 'traditional' standard de-normalisation patterns. In a sense, Data Warehouses already provide a Conformance Layer as their core set of structures - think of Snowflake schemas.

This is illustrated in figure 115.

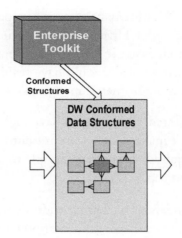

**Figure 115 – Conformed data structures in Data Warehouses**

But, we must remember that by enshrining the data's meaning in rigid structures, we already constrain the possible access variations of the data.

Some consumers will see this set of structures as problematic and so we may still need to provide a consumer-centric interpretation overlaying these core structures. As an example, maybe a consumer only ever requires a 'close of business' presentation of the data.

## Big Data Lakes

For Big Data Lakes, not only have few organisations created a Green Channel Ingestion Layer but they have no Conformance Layer either. Of course, in the absence of a Green Channel, this is not only a conceptual leap, but also a technologically difficult feat to deliver.

For these organisations, each reporting requirement has potentially resulted in a point solution. Each has created a separate set of structures, and often even technology stacks. We are all familiar with the concept of Data at Rest silos. But we can think of these as silo'd data flows. As a consequence, each of these has been unable to build on the work of any others, and each is almost certain to give varying answers to any given question.

We now know though that if we had adopted our Green Channel, there is a better path readily available to us.

Let's take a very simple Conformance Layer approach using HiveQL. We can carry out the mapping of Hive Tables to the underlying data sources. This exercise is *very* much easier if we have implemented the Green Channel as described earlier. This would have resulted in very much simpler and possibly semi-automated mappings.

Depending on the ingested data, we may have highly normalised data available. In this case, it makes sense to represent this in normalised HiveQL Tables. If required, it would be simple to add a de-normalised Conformance Layer on top.

This layer can pre-join data as well as provide standard core de-normalisation such as 'Organisation Formation Country Code'.

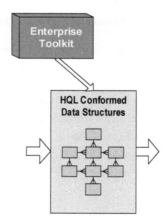

**Figure 116 – Conformed HQL data structures in Big Data Lakes**

## Master and Reference Data Alignment

What we haven't drawn attention to so far, is the Master data in our Consolidation Hubs.

If we think about the data in the Green Channel, we realise that Master Data will comprise a significant proportion of its Entities.

Traditionally, Data Warehouses have typically aligned the ingested data with Master and Reference data, prior to exposing it through their data structures to consumers. This data is largely represented through the Dimensions of the Data Warehouse structures.

Similarly Operational Data Stores have typically carried out a similar set of activities within their core structures. They have needed to do this to be able to consolidate the operational data to conformed meaning.

By contrast, this approach has often been omitted during the equivalent exercise involving a Big Data Lake.

Given the importance of conformed and regulated Master Data, it makes a lot of sense to ensure that we provide a 'Master Data as a Service' capability within our Conformed Layer.

## Consumer Layer

Many organisations are wrestling so hard with the ingestion of their data and absence of any conformed data structures that they have little resource left to concentrate on the primary purpose of the Hubs.

This forgotten purpose, is to provide a big-picture of our data to the Consolidation Hub's *consumers*.

As mentioned earlier, the Conformance Layer structures can *constrain* the styles of consumption due to their rigid structures.

> **Principle 174  The implementation of the structures in our Consolidation Hubs will have a radical effect on constraining the possible Consumer demands from them.**

This means that, for example, Star and Snowflake schemata may well prevent more operationally focussed consumers from getting the data they require.

Recently, I worked with a Client to mitigate exactly this constraint. Instead of a 'traditional' Warehouse set of structures, we created highly normalised Conformed Data Structures. We could ignore the performance constraints that this introduced, because, by today's standards, their transactional data volumes were low.

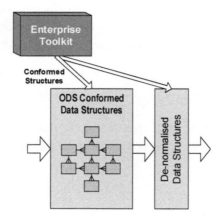

**Figure 117 – Consumer data structures in Operational Data Stores**

We then built a number of different styles of 'pre-canned' Consumer-centric Layers on top of these structures, as illustrated in figure 117. Each of these had markedly different purposes. Some were similar to traditional Warehouse structures, others less normalised and presenting an 'as at today' snapshot of the data.

Let's see how we need to approach getting the data to be consumer-focussed.

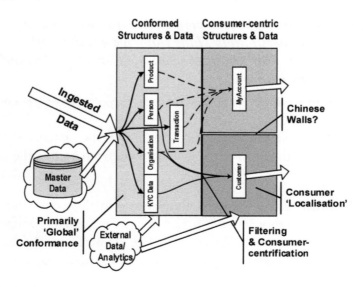

**Figure 118 – Data flows through the Conformance and Consumer Layers**

What we see in figure 118 is the Conformance Layer creating universal Entity definitions with conformance and limited de-normalisations. These support a wide range of Consumer Layer requirements.

We can also see two consumer-centric sections of the Consumer layer. Each have their own data structures[68], providing customisations specific to their consumers. Nonetheless, these rely on the Conformance Layer Entities as their basis, both for the definitions and the instantiated data sources.

Consider the following examples of the high-level benefits illustrated by figure 118:

| Feature | Benefits |
|---|---|
| Consumer defined Entities and Attribution | Fine-tuned support for consumer requirements, independent development and maintenance |
| Filtering on underlying data | Fine-tuned support for consumer requirements and efficiency of processing |
| Chinese walls capability | Implementing internal 'conflict of interest' and data access data segregation for any consumers |
| Augmentation by Localised additional data | Additional data for consumer-centric analysis |

Let's look at this flexible Consumer Layer approach in a little more detail.

## Enterprise Conformance Levels

We need to remind ourselves that the scope of our conformance is not a one size fits all. For many organisations, the data that truly fits into the core Enterprise-wide data scope can be quite small compared to their total data scope.

Typically, Lines of Business or Regional variations need to be taken into account. This reinforces the idea of GLocalisation, described in the 'Data Modelling' chapter. That is, we need to fully support both Global and Local data.

Figure 119 illustrates the idea that we will create high-level conformed Entities in the Conformance Layer. These are conformed at the highest level of 'consensus' applicable to *all* potential Consumer requirements.

---

68    For simplicity each area shows just one Entity. However, this number could vary from half a dozen up to several hundred.

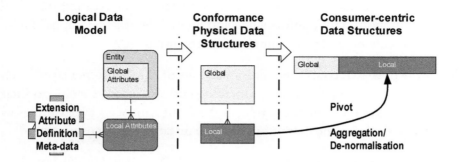

**Figure 119 – GLocalisation in the Conformance and Consumer Layers**

It may be difficult to determine these, but actually, if they conform to the Enterprise Data Model definitions of the High-level Entities[69], this would provide a good first-cut.

## Consumer Localisations

It is the job of the Consumer Layer to provide the Local variations to support each specific consumer's needs.

Typical examples of the variations include:

- Local Attribution

- Local Language

When we provide the data from the Consumer Layer, the ease of understanding and consumption is paramount. Typically this means we need to flatten the Localised data from rows into columns.

Let's examine a simple example as shown in figure 120.

---

69  Please refer to the cycle of normalisation on page 68.

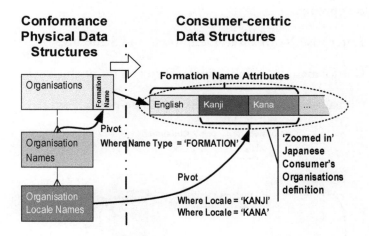

**Figure 120 – Pivoting local data**

What this schematic illustrates, is twofold:

1) In the Conformed Layer the Organisation's English 'Formation Name' is de-normalised into a conformed column. There should only be one of these per Organisation, so the de-normalisation should be valid. It is also a useful standard transformation, since many consumers will be interested in this core Organisation data. If this isn't built into the Conformance Layer, then the Joining and filtering it from the multiple rows of the Organisation Names data, offers a significant barrier for consumers.

2) In the Consumer Layer we can also see that a Japanese set of consumers require Kanji and Kana representations of the Organisation Formation Name. These have been pivoted and filtered into columns from the underlying Locale data. This illustrates the implementation of the GLocalisation approach we first encountered on page 58.

## Enterprise Data Models in Consolidation Hubs

We have seen that we need to use the Enterprise Data Models to ensure that the common understanding of our data pervades all implementations. This is as true for Consolidation Hubs as anywhere else.

Looking at figure 120, we see that we need to support the data structures in the Consumer Layer with the Enterprise Data Models. This will have a threefold approach:

1. Enterprise Normalised Definitions and Structures

2. Conformance – Global normalised and de-normalised

3. Consumer - Locally normalised and de-normalised

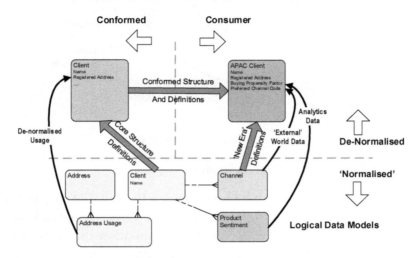

**Figure 121 – Enterprise Data Models scoping in Consolidation Hubs**

Let's discuss these in more detail in the following sections.

## Enterprise Normalised Definitions and Structures

We will often not be able to implement our normalised Logical Data Models directly using for example, a Relational Database. If we are using a File System like HDFS for the core data of our Consolidation Hub, then we need to be able to apply the *understanding* from our Logical Data Model, rather than creating actual data structures directly based upon it.

However, if we have used the ingestion Green Channel approach as described previously, we should be able to use the Logical Data Models as our blueprint for the structures and definitions.

## Conformed Globally and De-normalised

In the Conformance Layer, we must strive for structures that will form a 'universal' set of structures. To a great degree, these will depend on the scope of what we mean by universal. If universal translates to Enterprise, then the structures and definitions will need to be universally applicable across the Enterprise.

This means that the core structures will reflect the Enterprise Conceptual Model. We will also need to instantiate more localised data into this layer. This will make it available for the Consumer Layer specific data requirements.

In this part of the implemented Data Models, we have defined a degree of de-normalisation. Here we might see aggregation of core data such as 'Sales Revenue Year To Date'. Or possibly, 'qualified' de-normalisations like Organisation 'Formation Name'. But these must have a common pattern and not a Localised interpretation.

## Locally Conformed and De-normalised

Each Consumer may have very different criteria for their access to the Conformed Data Structures. They may not be interested in the entire universe of Entities, and even for those Entities that they do want to consume data, they may only want a sub-set of the Global Attributes.

But almost certainly they will then want to add in Localised Data structures and possibly Local Reference Domains, or Language interpretations of the data.

In addition to this, although the entire core data may encompass, say the Americas, the specific consumer may only be interested in Canadian data for their requirements. Hence the data sourced from the Conformed object/s, may also be filtered. This approach also provides a powerful mechanism to isolate consumers from seeing data they should not have access to. One set of requirements this supports is the need for internal 'conflict of interest' Chinese Walls.

Using this approach, we see that we can lower the 'barrier to entry' for new consumers to the Consolidation Hub. And, as a result, we have improved the agility for the organisation as a whole.

## Consumer Tool Agility

Many organisations are caught in the curse of modern times, whereby they have not finished evaluating one tool before the next one is released. This new tool boasts features so powerful and enhanced that the organisation feels compelled to start evaluating it!

This is nowhere more true than for consumer reporting tools. But adopting the new incarnations of these tools can be the exact antithesis of agility.

Many such tools have the capability to create a data object layer within the tool. The classic example for this being SAP® Business Objects 'Semantic Layer'. This layer is able to take the underlying data of a system and transform it in such a way as to become easier to report on, primarily because:

- Local Attribution Business meaning is incorporated into it and

- Complex normalised structures are replaced with simplified and intuitive datasets

This is all good.

However, what this book wants you to consider is a significant problem inherent in this approach. This problem is that the layer inside *each* such tool, requires development and maintenance.

This may, of course, demand specialist input. Because the resources may not have been involved in the data source delivery, their understanding of the data structures and patterns, may not be good. As a result, what they produce, can provide a less than perfect interpretation of the data and contain inconsistencies.

Additionally, such resources may be hard to come by and also be required infrequently. This can result in a 'starting from scratch', each time any changes are required.

Testing aims to remove some of these problems, but in my experience, this may still not resolve them satisfactorily. This can be due to the problems of communicating the understanding of the data to the testers, and other resourcing constraints, such as SME availability.

Should a new tool be chosen to replace the existing one, then the IP contained in the existing tool's layer will need to be 'ported' to the new tool. Often, it will need to return exactly the same reported data as before, with no reporting discontinuities allowed.

This may present quite a challenge, since:

- it is a different tool with different capabilities

- different Software Engineers may be developing it

- different understanding is now held by stakeholders

By comparison, if the reporting tool uses a defined Consumer Layer for its access, there is no need for complex transformations in it. All the new tool needs to do, is represent the Consumer Layer data, and this immediately transforms the set-up and maintenance costs of this tool.

The 'hard work' is being done in the Consumer Layer which was built by the original resources. As a result, it will have the IP correctly interpreted as a matter of course. In addition, it will have been thoroughly tested as part of the overall delivery testing.

> ***Principle 175*** ***Creating a Consumer Layer that can be queried by all consumers, including reporting tools, can radically improve the reporting consistency and reduce development and maintenance costs of the consumer.***

# 11: The Data Architect Blueprint

*Data Architects are the organisation's data champions who will drive and maximise its data agility and thus guarantee its ongoing success.*

The organisations that we work in are rarely perfect.

If we focus purely on their data realm, they are commonly beset by issues that act to obstruct good Data Architectural practice. It is the responsibility of the Data Architecture function to identify and overcome these impediments. The purpose of this book is to provide useful guidance that can be used to enhance this function.

So far, we have defined many of the features of the landscape in which the Data Architect role operates. But what are the characteristics of this role that will ensure its success within this landscape?

This chapter examines the patterns the Data Architect role requires, so that it can deliver on its responsibilities.

At the most basic level, a Data Architect needs to be able to absorb, challenge and distil understanding from often incomplete and contradictory testimony. However, this understanding is worthless unless it benefits the way the organisations operates in the use of its data. Their work needs to use this understanding, to influence the people and processes of the organisation, in order to maximise the positive outcomes it can derive from its data. Of course, this influence relies upon the Data Architect exhibiting thought-leadership and effective communication.

This chapter brings into focus all of the relevant principles, skills and techniques that have a direct bearing on making the Data Architect role become more effective.

## Abstraction Skills

Data Architecture is the organisational function that makes the chaos of the Real World's data fit into a well-managed, rational framework of meaning that enables the organisation to thrive. This framework can only be established and evolved through the recognition of patterns.

Abstraction is the skill that allows us to reveal inherent, but obscured patterns. Therefore, this skill is at the heart of the Data Architect's toolkit.

> **Principle 176  Abstraction is so fundamental to Data Architecture, that arguably in its absence, little of Data Architectural merit can be achieved!**

Listed below are several examples of the application of this skill.

## Abstraction in Data Modelling

Data modelling entails a set of thought processes and ways of working that create understanding beyond the data model itself. To an extent, data models can be seen as simply the *communication deliverables*, produced by effective use of abstraction and analytical skills.

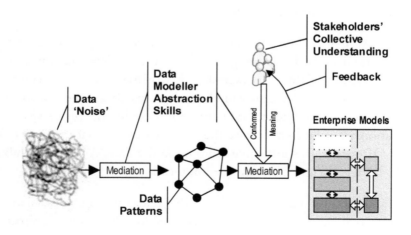

**Figure 122 – Data modelling abstraction skills**

The application of abstraction to raw evidence, is absolutely essential in order to develop crisp, well-formed definitions of the data Entities and record them in the Enterprise Data Models. This ability strips away instance specific aspects and deduces meaning and typing, to reveal a communicable understanding of the data's *meaning*.

> ***Principle 177*** **Data patterns can be deduced by filtering out the 'noise' and specificity of data occurrences.**

Also, abstraction is an absolute pre-requisite to be able to disambiguate synonymous terms, but also coalesce these where appropriate.

As a more immediately practical example, the data modelling chapter introduced the idea that simply *abstracting* names will increase the longevity of data models. This will improve the benefits derived from such models, by removing mechanisms and 'point in time' understanding from the data's meaning.

> ***Principle 178*** **Good data models require the application of abstraction and analytical skills to ensure their longevity and future-proofing.**

## Filling Gaps using Abstraction

Often its data is not well defined *anywhere* within our organisations.

What definitions do exist, are often dispersed across multiple repositories, intranet sites, or held in obscure, architect-only and unmaintained repository definitions. Sometimes, we will even stumble across a spreadsheet 'data model' on someone's desktop!

Unsurprisingly, within such an environment, liberating the full potential and understanding of an organisation's data, is often a significant challenge.

The Data Architect needs to be able to discover patterns and meaning from (often) poorly structured sources. Gaps in sources require special consideration. Data Architects need to use their abstraction skills in conjunction with their intuition and experience, to detect and plug any such gaps. They must also work closely with SMEs, to help identify, verify and remediate any gaps in understanding. This teamwork is critical to improve the reliability of any analysis.

## Abstraction in Data Analysis

Data Analysis skills can be characterised as discovering patterns in data and then creating hypotheses based upon them that can be evaluated by further investigation. Thus, the fundamental skill for any forensic analysis of data is abstraction. This skill is often required in order to adequately define a problem domain.

## Abstraction in Scoping Requirements

In the absence of Data Architectural input, requirements typically deliver point solutions. It is a prime responsibility of a Data Architect to consider beyond the scope of the current requirements.

> *Principle 179  If a Data Architect is driven only by requirements, then they are not truly acting within the realm of Data Architecture!*

This is illustrated by figure 123.

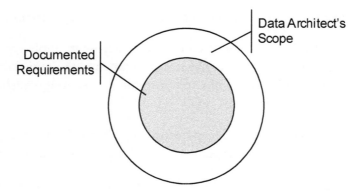

Documented Requirements

Data Architect's Scope

**Figure 123 – Data Architect's scope**

Immediate requirements help bound the scope of change, but Data Architects always need to consider beyond this scope.

In part, to be able to do this requires an abstraction ability. It is only by abstraction that any constraints imposed by the immediate requirements can be removed, delivering future-proofed definitions.

> ***Principle 180*** *** Abstracting beyond the 'now', provides an organisation with a degree of protection for its un-knowable future.***

## Abstraction in Decision Making

Earlier in the 'Agile Data Assurance' chapter, we described the crucial role played by abstracted principles. In order to work out which abstracted principles to apply in any given situation, a Data Architect must possess the ability to apply abstraction to any given problem domain.

> ***Principle 181*** *** Abstraction of problem definitions is a pre-requisite for any decision-making that relies on abstracted principles.***

## Predicting the Future

Predicting the future is always a handy skill!

Unfortunately, there are not many of us who can do it. So if this is a key skill, what can the Data Architect do in the absence of being gifted to foretell the future?

A simple technique is to vigorously probe all the boundaries of problem specifications. Of particular interest is, how *real* the bases for any constraints and assumptions are. It is worth concentrating initially on the constraints and assumptions that are mechanistic, since these are the most certain to change over time. Additionally, consider those governed by legislation or regulations, since these are certain to need to respond to future changes in their respective frameworks.

Constraints and assumptions are rarely immutable, and even though others have provided assertions that they are, the Data Architect should always discover their true origin, in order to be satisfied of their validity.

> **Principle 182  Removing constraints and challenging any assumptions driven by the 'now', yields a degree of resilience for the organisation to face its unknowable future.**

In my experience, almost all constraints and assumptions that were initially stated as immutable, have proved to be changeable. However, it may be wise to keep any scepticism to yourself, until you have verified their validity or otherwise. Alienating yourself from stakeholders is a costly mistake that is not easy to remedy later!

As a part of testing whether boundaries may be subject to future changes, use can be made of trends that are in the areas of operation of an organisation. Many of these themes are common across organisations including, for instance:

- technical innovation
- legislative and regulatory changes
- internal reorganisation
- off-shoring/outsourcing
- macro and micro economic climates that impact the organisation
- Big Data adoption

And increasingly:

- Micro-services delivery

- Cloud adoption

- AI and Machine Learning

- Blockchain

- Internet of Things

## Technical Skills

A working knowledge of some technical skills, for example, SQL and JSON, is extremely useful, as these tend to be used across many data systems.

> **Principle 183** *The Data Architect needs to possess at least some technical ability, since they need to straddle the technical and non-technical domains.*

In particular, SQL can be useful for example for carrying out ad hoc queries associated with detailed data analysis in many databases[70].

In addition, a degree of proficiency with a wide range of communication tools such as; modelling tools, diagramming tools, word processing, spreadsheets and presentation tools, are vital for successful communication. This communication is essential if a Data Architect is to have any impact on an organisation.

## Personality Profile

This section contains details of personality traits that I have seen exhibited by highly effective Data Architects.

### Goal-Driven

Goal-driven refers to thinking of data benefit *across* the Enterprise and *beyond* the immediate requirements and implementations.

---

70   Even big data has SQL type interfaces, such as Apache Hive™.

> **Principle 184** *The Data Architect needs to be driven by goals and not tasks.*

Of course, Data Architects need to complete tasks. But they must never think of each of these in isolation, and always have universality in mind. Thus, the execution of their tasks must always be aligned with their goals.

For a Data Architect, it is important to recognise that, whilst they need to complete tasks, their goals are rarely achievable. This is due to the constantly shifting Data Architectural landscape.

## Solution-Oriented

In my experience, solutions are normally revealed as a result of successfully bounding the specification of the problem.

This is harder than it sounds, but by exploring the envelope of the problem and probing which constraints and assumptions bound it, potential ways to solve it often become clear!

> **Principle 185** *To reveal solutions, Data Architects need to bound problems, but never become problem-bound!*

These possible solutions can then be evaluated to define the best approach for the organisation.

The Data Architect needs to see a complete and concise problem definition as a step towards the solution. However, they must never focus on the problem for its own sake.

## Detail-Oriented

To have an overall understanding of an organisation's data, it is often beneficial to *not* understand the *minutiae* in *all areas*. However, when drilling down to specifics, the ability to switch to a detail-oriented way of thinking is often essential.

> **Principle 186** **A Data Architect must be able to be detail-oriented when required.**

Probing details is not always a popular activity, but if used to the right level, in the right areas, the benefits can be dramatic as indicated by the idiom 'the devil is always in the detail!'

## Big-Picture Oriented

Not only must the Data Architect be able to be detail-oriented, but they must also always see any detail within the context of the big-picture.

> **Principle 187** **Data Architects must have the big-picture in their minds at all times.**

All of the minutiae need to have coherence within the whole, and without this sensitivity it is questionable whether a person can truly be a Data Architect.

## Open Minded

It is always tempting to think that you have the right answer and therefore to dismiss any communications that contradict this.

Many times I have learned that *my right* answer was actually missing some key information. This has sometimes meant that it was not as correct as I had previously thought!

Also, consider that by having an open mind, you tend to encourage this behaviour in others. This allows you to achieve mutually beneficial working relationships with other stakeholders.

---

**Principle 188**   *Data Architects must have an open mind to evolve the best solutions and to build effective working relationships.*

---

In addition, don't become emotionally attached to a particular solution. This can blind you to other potential solutions, and possibly alienate you from other stakeholders. It can also taint relationships with negative emotions, leading to a loss of trust, confidence and consensus.

---

**Principle 189**   *Data Architects must never become emotionally attached to solutions, as this can lead to conflict, and a loss of trust and influence with other stakeholders.*

---

## Thought-Leader

Thought-leadership is a key trait that provides the influence that the Data Architect role requires in order to deliver change within an organisation.

---

**Principle 190**   *The Data Architect needs to be a thought-leader in order to transform an organisation's benefit from its data.*

---

To be a thought-leader, relies on building consensus, and shared goals, values and standards – otherwise you are just having 'thoughts'. These characteristics are in contrast to the often held misconception that great Data Architecture equates to simply producing high quality artefacts.

> *Principle 191* **In the absence of transforming the way that stakeholders think, even perfect artefacts will provide negligible benefit to an organisation.**

Some other personal qualities to think about that will help in the quest to become a thought leader, are being:

- determined

- approachable

- didactic

- fair

- consistent

- non-judgemental

Pre-eminent in the value system that a Data Architect needs to disseminate is a positive, solution oriented attitude.

Being a visionary is also an excellent characteristic. But the Data Architect must never forget not to go too far, too fast, which can sometimes risk them losing touch with other stakeholders whose support they need.

## Team Player

I have learned over the years to evolve solutions within well-focussed groups, as these have always delivered far superior outcomes.

> *Principle 192* **Data Architects need to establish positive team work in their relationships with all stakeholders.**

To build an effective team in which they operate the Data Architect should:

- promote joint ownership

- cultivate trust and respect

- always use individual strengths in the team to cover individual weaknesses

- never be afraid to admit that others have valuable contributions to make

- always provide positive feedback and support as a matter of course

## Communication Expert

Effective communication skills for a Data Architect are typically seen as being able to produce high quality documentation. But this emphasis will never in itself result in a Data Architect carrying out a transformational role.

---

**Principle 193** *Without effective communication skills, a Data Architect can only be of limited use to an organisation.*

---

Returning to the communication model introduced in chapter 1 and adding in the principle of individual Awareness Sets of knowledge, experience and behaviours, we can develop the following model.

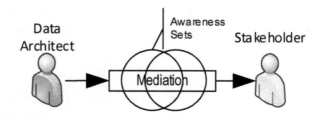

**Figure 124 – Data Architect as a communication expert**

To improve communication effectiveness, the Data Architect should consider the techniques described in the following sections.

## Audience-centric Communication

Prior to *any* interaction, think about the audience.

For example, consider their: expertise, knowledge, cultural background, personality traits and individual agendas, and modify your message and dissemination mechanism accordingly.

> *Principle 194* **All communications need to be Audience-centric to maximise their effectiveness.**

This approach will allow you to mediate your messages to accommodate the Awareness Sets of your audience. Try to make audiences reasonably homogenous and aligned to the purpose of the communication. As a result of these simple techniques, you will find that your messages are immeasurably more effective.

## Tailor Documents to suit the Audience

When formal interactions are based upon material such as presentation decks or other documents, review the material critically to ensure it is fit for purpose. This is especially important when you are intending to use material that was created earlier for a different audience.

## Echo and Replay

Use the techniques of echoing back what you think was just conveyed by other stakeholders, or getting others to replay what they think you have just communicated to them.

> *Principle 195* **Echo and Replay can be used to establish that effective communication has taken place, with common understanding and agreement.**

Figure 125 illustrates Principle 195 schematically.

**Figure 125 – Echo and Replay to test communication**

Always use emails, or other similar techniques, to summarise significant outcomes from meetings, and always invite correction in these.

## Novel Term Injection

This is a great technique for introducing and gaining common acceptance of concepts. The way it works is like this; think of a term that describes principles or approaches around which you wish to establish common understanding and agreement.

***Principle 196***    ***By modifying the stakeholder's vocabulary, the Data Architect's ideas will become part of the shared conceptual landscape.***

For example think of these terms:

- Event-driven lifecycle

- Trusted Source Accreditation

Start to repeatedly use your terms in any communications.

Then assess whether the term is being adopted by other stakeholders in their interactions, either with the Data Architect, and/or (hopefully) with each other.

The adoption of Novel Terms is a sure indication that there is an adoption of the concepts that underpin them.

> *Principle 197*    *Novel Term injection can be an effective technique to align thoughts and verify their adoption within an organisation.*

## Whiteboard Technology

If we consider the way of sharing ideas that whiteboards enable, it is clear why they are so important. The rapidity with which concepts, solutions and explanations can be created, and then reconfigured, provides true conceptual agility. In my opinion, there are no other technologies that come near to competing with whiteboards, when we consider these aspects.

> *Principle 198*    *Whiteboards are possibly the most effective (and underestimated) technology that the Data Architect can use.*

They are especially effective for rapidly putting together the first cuts, or amendments to all sorts of models, including those destined to become part of the Enterprise Data Models.

The Data Architect needs to become proficient in using whiteboard techniques to establish shared understanding and gain consensus, particularly around ways to move forward.

> *Principle 199*    *To be effective, Whiteboard techniques rely on the clarity of diagrams and text depicted on them.*

I have also noticed that the seemingly trivial act of passing the pens to stakeholders to record their ideas on the whiteboard, delivers a dramatic improvement in the shared ownership of the area being considered!

## Global Communications - The Tyranny of Distance

It never ceases to amaze me how even small separations between team members can cause a significant degradation of communication and productive work practises. Even working on another bank of desks, the other side of the floor, different floors or buildings, can dramatically reduce the effectiveness of team dynamics.

This is exacerbated significantly by geographic separation, which may also be compounded by differences in time zones, cultures and first languages.

---

*Principle 200   Lack of proximity of team members can have a profoundly negative impact on their effectiveness.*

---

We like to think that by using messengers, emails, conference calls and holding meetings (particularly scrums), we are able to somehow mitigate the effect of separation. But in my experience, although they may help, they rarely produce the equivalent advantages delivered by proximity.

Agile and DevOps methodologies mandate co-location as a cornerstone of their approach. I am convinced that just this in itself must produce a significant boost to communication, cross-skilling and the quality of delivery.

When working in teams that are dispersed geographically, you may want to consider the following as examples of changes that may assist with the way you work:

1. Use pictures in artefacts rather than words – these don't need as much translation (hopefully!)

2. If workflows cross time zones, instead of a normal turnaround for a task of say 1 hour, a day may now be required, so take this into account when planning

3. Use communicator groups or other software tools to facilitate baton handovers where complex processes or workflows are involved

4. Put more detail in emails and other transient communications than you would otherwise provide – to wait a day for a reply that asks for more clarification, can slow processes down to a snail's pace

5. Use Virtual Whiteboards to provide rapid prototyping and sharing of ideas

## Lower the Communication 'Barrier to Entry'

Smothering a document in highly technical terms, or providing a 100 page overview, will almost certainly prevent its meaning from being transferred to all but a limited audience.

> *Principle 201   Data Architects need to lower the communication 'barrier to entry' for concepts that they are trying to embed in the organisation.*

Also, consider that even if your audience are very busy, they would typically be willing to attend a walkthrough of your documents, rather than devote the same amount of time to reviewing them in isolation[71]. For some stakeholders, attaching document links to meeting requests as background reading, can pay big dividends, as they may want to avoid being 'on the back foot' in a meeting.

## Process rather than Artefacts

Artefacts are normally seen as the way to communicate understanding, but is this true?

Artefacts *do* provide a communication tool, but when we think about message mediation, we can see that they are far from perfect for this purpose.

---

71   See the next section.

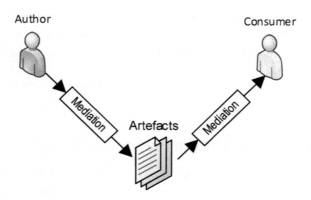

**Figure 126 – Chinese whispers**

When considering the information flows that Data Architects require, passively reading documents is rarely the best use of their time – this approach will *never* reveal *any* of the details, assumptions and constraints that are *absent* from them.

> **Principle 202** **Many constraints and assumptions are not explicitly stated anywhere, but often drop out of discussions.**

The *active* participation by a Data Architect is critical.

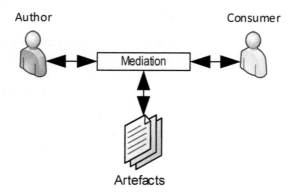

**Figure 127 – "Let me walk you through it …"**

Active sessions with stakeholders are far more productive and create consensus and shared ownership, leading to far better outcomes for all endeavours.

## Active Alignment

The Data Architect needs to use *processes* rather than relying on *artefacts* to *align stakeholders* with the overall goals. This will bring them 'on the journey', which results in collective ownership and therefore an easier transition to the target model.

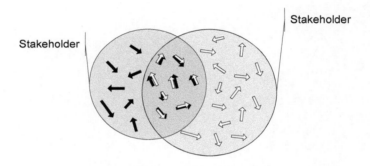

**Figure 128 – Aligning stakeholders**

This approach will also ensure that there will be no *surprises* when milestones and deliverables are communicated to stakeholders.

> *Principle 203*    ***Processes are infinitely more effective than passive artefacts at aligning stakeholders with: each other, requirements and corresponding deliverables.***

# A: Principle References

This Appendix provides a summary of the Key Points contained in the book.

# B: Figure References

This Appendix provides a summary of the Figures contained in the book.

# C: **About The Author**

Dave is a senior Enterprise Data Architect, with over 30 years of experience in the IT industry and over 15 years of experience of Data Architecture as a discipline. His experience has been gained by working across all business sectors and across the globe.

He has also created and managed two successful Oracle consultancies in London and Sydney Australia. From these he spun off various successful web ventures.

In parallel to acting as a consultant, he also has a strong background in education. This includes technical and business training for thousands of students through Oracle, its partners and tailored workshops for a wide range of Clients.

He currently works as a Consultant Enterprise Data Architect and more recently has developed course material and lectures for Universities in the UK and US.

A few years ago he started to author a popular series of books on Data Architecture Fundamentals and you might find that these two are useful companions to this book:

**The Data Model Toolkit – ISBN: 978-1782224730**

**True Agility From Agile+DevOps - ISBN: 978-1782225225**

There is also further material available on **thedatapoint.net** that you might also find useful.

Lightning Source UK Ltd.
Milton Keynes UK
UKHW020617231219
355886UK00005B/666/P